50 WALKS IN

Berkshire & Buckinghamshire

50 WALKS OF 2–10 MILES

First published 2002
Researched and written by Nick Channer
Field checked and updated 2008 by Martin Andrew
Series Management: Bookwork Creative Associates
Series Editors: Sandy Draper and Marilynne Lanng
Series Design Concept: Elizabeth Baldin and Andrew Milne
Designer: Elizabeth Baldin
Picture Research: Vivien Little
Proofreader: Pamela Stagg
Cartography provided by the Mapping Services Department of AA Publishing

Produced by AA Publishing
© Automobile Association Developments Limited 2009

Published by AA Publishing (a trading name of Automobile Association Developments Limited,
whose registered office is Fanum House, Basing View, Basingstoke, Hampshire RG21 4EA;
registered number 1878835)

Enabled by [OS Ordnance Survey] This product includes mapping data licensed from the Ordnance
Survey® with the permission of the Controller of Her Majesty's
Stationery Office. © Crown Copyright 2009. All rights reserved. Licence number 100021153.

A03627

ISBN: 978-0-7495-6047-8

A CIP catalogue record for this book is available from the British Library.

The contents of this book are believed correct at the time of printing. Nevertheless, the
publishers cannot be held responsible for any errors or omissions or for changes in the
details given in this book or for the consequences of any reliance on the information it
provides. This does not affect your statutory rights. We have tried to ensure accuracy in this
book, but things do change and we would be grateful if readers would advise us of any
inaccuracies they may encounter.

We have taken all reasonable steps to ensure that these walks are safe and achievable by
walkers with a realistic level of fitness. However, all outdoor activities involve a degree of risk
and the publishers accept no responsibility for any injuries caused to readers whilst following
these walks. For more advice on walking safely see page 144. The mileage range shown on the
front cover is for guidance only – some walks may be less than or exceed these distances.

Visit AA Publishing at www.aatravelshop.com

Colour reproduction by Keenes Group, Andover
Printed by Printer Trento Srl, Italy

Acknowledgements
The Automobile Association would like to thank the following photographers, companies and
picture libraries for their assistance in the preparation of this book.

Abbreviations for the picture credits are as follows: (AA) AA World Travel Library.

3 AA/M Moody; 9 AA/M Moody; 16/17 AA/C Jones; 46/47 AA/M Moody; 62/63 AA/V Bates;
82/83 AA/J A Tims; 99 AA/M Moody; 100 AA/M Moody; 110/111 AA/M Moody; 136/137 AA/M
Moody

Every effort has been made to trace the copyright holders, and we apologise in advance for
any accidental errors. We would be happy to apply the corrections in the following edition
of this publication.

Right: Pangbourne Meadow and the Thames (Walk 37)

AA

50 WALKS IN

Berkshire & Buckinghamshire

50 WALKS OF 2–10 MILES

Contents

Contents

Rating

Each walk is rated for its relative difficulty compared to the other walks in this book. Walks marked +++ are likely to be shorter and easier with little total ascent. The hardest walks are marked +++

Walking in Safety

For advice and safety tips see page 144.

Locator Map

Legend

—→—	Walk Route		Built-up Area
1	Route Waypoint		Woodland Area
— — —	Adjoining Path	👥	Toilet
🔆	Viewpoint	P	Car Park
•	Place of Interest	⊞	Picnic Area
⛰	Steep Section	)(	Bridge

Introducing Berkshire and Buckinghamshire

The adjoining counties of Berkshire and Buckinghamshire have long been recognised as two of England's prettiest shires. Classically English in their beauty and character, they reflect the best of our countryside. Their delightful mix of beech woodland, rolling farmland, quiet waterways and breezy downland, conspiring to represent some of the finest walking country in Britain. As with many other counties, Berkshire and Buckinghamshire are blessed with many miles of public rights of way, and the routes chosen for this guide reach deep into their rural heartlands, taking advantage of a rich legacy of historic sites and fascinating landmarks.

Buckinghamshire

Buckinghamshire is the larger of the two counties – its shape often compared to a lion rampant. This is a land of glorious beech trees, wide views and imposing country houses. The Victorian Prime Minister Benjamin Disraeli, who held office twice, savoured the peace and tranquillity of Hughenden Manor, while generations of statesmen have entertained politicians and world leaders at Chequers, the Prime Minister's rural retreat. Stowe and Waddesdon Manor are fine examples of even grander houses, amid sumptuous gardens and dignified parkland.

The Vale of Aylesbury is a vast playground with 1,000 miles (1,609km) of paths and tracks to explore. Rising above it like protective guardians are the Chiltern Hills, a designated Area of Outstanding Natural Beauty covering 308sq miles (880sq km). They are best appreciated in autumn when the leaves of the beech trees turn from dark green to deep brown. In the south-east corner of the Chilterns lie the woodland rides of Burnham Beeches, another haven for ramblers, wildlife lovers and those seeking peaceful recreation away from the noise and bustle of the city.

Buckinghamshire's history is long and eventful, but the county is also associated with events within living memory. At Bletchley Park, 60 years ago, more than 10,000 people worked in complete secrecy to try and bring a swift conclusion to the Second World War. Further south, an otherwise unremarkable stretch of railway line was made infamous by the Great Train Robbery in the summer of 1963.

Berkshire

Berkshire, too, has much to attract the walker. The county essentially consists of two distinct parts. The western half is predominantly rural, with the Lambourn Downs spilling down to the River Lambourn and the Berkshire Downs to the more majestic Thames. The eastern half of Berkshire may be more urban

PUBLIC TRANSPORT

Berkshire and Buckinghamshire are well served by public transport, making many of the walks in this guide easily accessible. For information about local bus services contact the Traveline on 0870 608 2608. Walks 2, 3, 15, 25, 30, 33, 36, 37 and 45 start at or near a railway station. For times of trains throughout the country call the 24-hour national train inquiry line on 08457 48 49 50. For countrywide public transport information look at the internet site www.pti.org.uk.

but here, too, there is the opportunity to get out and savour open spaces. Windsor Great Park and Maidenhead Thicket are prime examples.

Waterways and Towns

Threading their way through the county are two of the south's prettiest rivers – the Lambourn and the Pang. Beyond the tranquil tow paths of the Kennet and Avon Canal, Greenham Common's famous airbase has been transformed to delight walkers.

Towns and cities are a feature of this book, too. The sleepy backwaters of Reading provide a fascinating insight into how the town developed, while a tour of Milton Keynes demonstrates a bold step in city planning. Each route offers a specific theme to enhance the walk, as well as snippets of useful information on what to look for and what to do while you're there. Most are circular, though some require a train to return to the start. Enjoy the walks and savour the delights of Berkshire and Buckinghamshire's countryside.

Using this book

INFORMATION PANELS

An information panel for each walk shows its relative difficulty (see page 5), the distance and total amount of ascent. An indication of the gradients you will encounter is shown by the rating ▲ ▲ ▲ (no steep slopes) to ▲ ▲ ▲ (several very steep slopes).

MAPS

There are 30 maps, covering 40 of the walks. Some walks have a suggested option in the same area. The information panel for these walks will tell you how much extra walking is involved. On short-cut suggestions the panel will tell you the total distance if you set out from the start of the main walk. Where an option returns to the same point on the main walk, just the distance of the loop is given. Where an option leaves the main walk at one point and returns to it at another, then the distance shown is for the whole walk. The minimum time suggested is for reasonably fit walkers and doesn't allow for stops. Each walk has a suggested map.

START POINTS

The start of each walk is given as a six-figure grid reference prefixed by two letters indicating which 100km square of the National Grid it refers to. You'll find more information on grid references on most Ordnance Survey maps.

DOGS

We have tried to give dog owners useful advice about how dog friendly each walk is. Please respect other countryside users. Keep your dog under control, especially around livestock, and obey local bylaws and other dog control notices.

CAR PARKING

Many of the car parks suggested are public, but occasionally you may find you have to park on the roadside or in a lay-by. Please be considerate when you leave your car, ensuring that access roads or gates are not blocked and that other vehicles can pass safely.

Right: The view from Beacon Hill (Walk 13/14)

Stowe's Fair, Majestic Paradise

*Savour the delights of Stowe, with its famous
18th-century landscape garden and surrounding parkland.*

DISTANCE 4.5 miles (7.2km) **MINIMUM TIME** 2hrs

ASCENT/GRADIENT Negligible ▲▲▲ **LEVEL OF DIFFICULTY** ✦✦✦

PATHS Field paths, estate drives, stretches of road, 3 stiles

LANDSCAPE Farmland and parkland

SUGGESTED MAP OS Explorer 192 Buckingham & Milton Keynes

START / FINISH Grid reference: SP 684357

DOG FRIENDLINESS Under control across farmland, on lead within Stowe Park

PARKING On-street parking in Chackmore

PUBLIC TOILETS Stowe Landscape Garden

Stowe has been described as England's greatest work of art and possibly the world's most bewitching landscape garden. But how did it all begin? It was Sir Richard Temple (1634–97), one of Marlborough's generals and described as 'the greatest Whig in the army', who first built a brick mansion here. Work eventually came to an end in 1839 when Stowe's then owner, the 2nd Duke of Buckingham, a descendant of Lord Cobham, suffered financial problems and was declared bankrupt.

Temple's son (1669–1749, also Sir Richard) married a wealthy brewery heiress, became Lord, and later Viscount Cobham and began to extend the house and park. He prided himself on his reputation as a great radical – anti-Stuart and pro-liberty, greatly endorsing the ideals of the Glorious Revolution. Although work on the gardens at Stowe started in 1711, it wasn't until Lord Cobham fell out with the George II and his Prime Minister, Robert Walpole, that the idea of an experiment in 'moral gardening' really seized him.

Cobham threw himself wholeheartedly into the project. His aim was to create a garden of ideas; a place symbolising the notion of liberty. Historians maintain that Cobham was attempting to rewrite the history of Britain, using buildings and landscape.

Many Hands

In 1713 Stowe employed only half a dozen garden staff, but five years later there were almost 30 gardeners. Work at Stowe became a way of life, and so anxious was Cobham for the momentum not to be broken that, when his head gardener Edward Bissell broke his leg, he called for a specially adapted chair so that Bissell could continue to work.

In total, Cobham designed eight lakes, constructed more than three dozen temples, and commissioned 50 statues and 40 busts. The country's finest artists and designers, including James Gibbs, William Kent and Sir John Vanbrugh, were employed to help create what James Thomson described as 'the fair majestic paradise of Stowe'. Even Lancelot 'Capability' Brown had a hand in it, beginning his career here in 1741.

STOWE

Lord Cobham's successors consolidated his work by improving and adding to the garden. However, by the mid-19th century, the family fortunes had ebbed away and the estate was sold. After a further sale in 1921, Cobham's vision of an earthly paradise, described by Alexander Pope as 'a work to wonder at', was left virtually empty. The house became a school and the National Trust acquired the garden in 1989.

WALK 1 DIRECTIONS

❶ Walk through Chackmore, pass the Queen's Head, and continue through the village. At the speed derestriction signs, keep ahead for a few paces and look for a path on the left. Aim diagonally right in the field, passing under power lines.

Make for a stile beneath the branches of an oak tree in the corner where waymarks indicate that the path forks.

❷ Cross the field towards two stiles, making for the one on the left, beyond which is a plank bridge. Keep to the right boundary of an elongated field

WALK 1

and when it widens, go diagonally right to the far corner. Stowe Castle is over to the right, and to the left the outline of the Corinthian Arch is just visible among the trees. Through a gate join a path, pass under telegraph wires and look for a gap and waymark ahead. Walk ahead and descend to footbridge.

WHAT TO LOOK OUT FOR

The triangular Gothic Temple, used by the Landmark Trust as a holiday let, can be seen from the walk, as can Stowe Castle, a remarkable eye-catcher built in the 18th century. Look out, too, for the Bourbon Tower, which was built in the 1740s as a gamekeeper's lodge in iron-rich Northamptonshire limestone and given an octagonal turret in 1845.

❸ Over the stream and through a gate go into the field and head up the slope, keeping to the left of two distant houses. Head for a single-storey dwelling in the top corner and as you climb the slope, the outline of the Gothic Temple looms into view. Go through a galvanised gate by a lodge at Lamport and continue ahead on the bridleway. The Bourbon Tower is clearly visible over to the right. Pass through a gate and keep ahead towards an obelisk monument commemorating the Duke of Buckingham. Merge with another path and keep a sports ground on your right.

❹ Make for a gate leading out to the left of an avenue of trees running down towards the Grecian Valley. Cross over and follow the track on the right hand side of the ha-ha up to a clump of trees. Bear left here and follow the wide avenue, part of a Roman road. Pass the National Trust entrance building and shop

WHILE YOU'RE THERE

The walk skirts the garden, offering good views of its classical features. Stowe is very large and visitors often allow most of the day for a leisurely tour. One of Stowe's most popular features is the Grecian Valley, overlooked by the Temple of Concorde and Victory. The valley was 'Capability' Brown's first large-scale design and consists of a lovely sloping glade with vistas towards monuments of Lord Cobham and General Wolfe.

and then the magnificent façade of Stowe School and keep along the main drive. On reaching the Boycott Pavilions, branch off half left along track to a stile by the cattle grid and sign for the Corinthian Arch. Down below lies the Oxford Water, crossed by a splendid 18th-century stone bridge.

❺ Follow the drive through the parkland with glimpses of temples and classical designs. The drive eventually reaches the Corinthian Arch. Line up with the arch and pause here to absorb the breathtaking view of Stowe School, surely one of Britain's stateliest vistas. Walk down the avenue to the road junction, swing left and return to Chackmore.

WHERE TO EAT AND DRINK

The Queen's Head in Chackmore offers a range of traditional beers, including Banks. There is also a beer garden and a choice of meals and snacks – ranging from baguettes and chilli to lasagne and steak and kidney pudding. There is a licensed tea room at Stowe, serving morning coffee, light lunches and afternoon tea. A children's menu is also available. Alternatively, bring a picnic – permitted only in the Grecian Valley.

A Tour of Milton Keynes, City of the Future

See how a brand-new city has been shaped and styled on this unique walk with a strong architectural theme.

DISTANCE 3.5 miles (5.7km)	**MINIMUM TIME** 2hrs
ASCENT/GRADIENT Negligble ▲▲▲	**LEVEL OF DIFFICULTY** ✦✦✦
PATHS Paved walkways, boulevards and park paths	
LANDSCAPE City centre and park	
SUGGESTED MAP OS Explorer 192 Milton Keynes & Buckingham, or street map from tourist information centre	
START / FINISH Grid reference: SP 842380	
DOG FRIENDLINESS Probably not most dogs' idea of fun	
PARKING Car park at Milton Keynes Station	
PUBLIC TOILETS Milton Keynes Station and shopping centres	

Much has happened to Milton Keynes since 1967 when an area of almost 22,000 acres (8,910ha) was designated for the construction of a new city. But why Milton Keynes? The planners and architects of the day considered its location at the heart of England to be just about perfect. Centrally positioned within the country, only an hour from London by car on the new M1 motorway and easily accessible by train, the city's communication links were seen as ideal.

The First Settlers

It was in around 2000 BC that people first settled here and the remains of the earliest known house in the area date back to the late Bronze Age or early Iron Age. Later, the Romans occupied this part of the country, their farms and rural settlements were served by two towns – Lactodorum and Magiovinium. Near by ran Watling Street, now the A5, linking London, the West Midlands and North Wales.

During the 19th century the Milton Keynes area of Buckinghamshire began to expand, largely due to the dawning of the railway era that brought industrial prosperity to places like Newport Pagnell and Wolverton. The opening of the M1 in 1959 sealed the area's future as the site of a new city required to meet the demands of the business world and its employees, and accommodating a quarter of a million people within its boundaries. The task of housing a growing population became a priority and, as the 20th century drew to a close, attention was focused on Milton Keynes as the place to live and work.

The Birth of a New City

Richard Crossman, Minister of Housing and Local Government (1964–66) supported the plan for a new city. Initially it was envisaged that Milton Keynes would consist of high-density settlements connected by monorail to a commercial centre – an innovative move and a far cry from the old concept of garden suburbs as developed by the London planners. However, the monorail system was eventually shelved in favour of a dispersed network of housing within a grid pattern of roads.

With its tree-lined boulevards, green squares and stylish office buildings, it's hard not to be impressed by Milton Keynes. It may get a bad press in some quarters, and there are those who feel it has too strong an American influence, but the city has been designed with convenience, mobility and modern living in mind. There are many who say it works.

WALK 2 DIRECTIONS

❶ With your back to the station, aim slightly left, line up with a row of flag-poles and make for two underpasses. Keep ahead along Midsummer Boulevard, passing the sculpture on the left. Make for the next subway and cross Witan Gate and Upper 5th Street. Swing left just before the next subway to visit the domed Church of Christ the Cornerstone. Keep the church on your left and continue to Silbury Boulevard, passing under the subway ahead.

MILTON KEYNES

WALK 2

WHAT TO LOOK OUT FOR

Milton Keynes likes to compete at the cutting edge of modern architecture. Equip yourself with information leaflets about the city and head off in search of a host of unusual buildings and eye-catching sculptures. One building to look out for is The Point, which opened in 1985, and takes the form of a striking 70ft (21m) high, mirror-sided ziggurat (a rectangular stepped tower) upon which a red tubular pyramid structure has been superimposed.

2 Turn right through a subway and pass Milton Keynes Library and Exhibition Gallery. Pass North 9th Street and a statue of the Lloyds black horse at Lloyds Court. Swing right and pass under the road to approach the shopping centre at Deer Walk. Don't enter the complex here, but instead turn left and walk along to the next entrance, numbered 11, at Eagle Walk. Go straight through, pass a map of the shopping centre and emerge at Entrance 12, Midsummer Boulevard.

3 Turn left to Field Walk and turn right here to cross the boulevard. Bear left to reach the tourist information centre, Milton Keynes Theatre and the city's

WHILE YOU'RE THERE

Visit the Church of Christ the Cornerstone – the first purpose-built ecumenical city centre church in Britain. The church is 101ft (31m) high, to the top of the lantern, while the cross rises a further 18ft (5m), making it the highest point in the city. Surrounding the church is a cloister and adjacent is the Guildhall, a meeting place for business and commerce in Milton Keynes.

gallery. Continue ahead under the subway and cross the footbridge into Campbell Park. Skirt the round pond and make for the beacon that represents the highest point in the park. As you approach it, turn sharp right and follow the path as it snakes down through the park. Roughly 30yds (27m) before a circular seat bear sharp right to join a grassy path alongside a fence. Make for a second kissing gate and turn right. Walk along to the next path junction, with a kissing gate on the right. Turn left here, back towards the centre of Milton Keynes. Keep to the left to join a wide concrete ride and follow the waymarked city centre route.

WHERE TO EAT AND DRINK

There are plenty of café bars and restaurants in Milton Kenyes, providing a wide-ranging choice of food and drink. Midsummer Place shopping complex offers a particularly good selection.

4 Turn right to cross the road bridge to Bankfield roundabout and go straight ahead along Avebury Boulevard. Cross Secklow Gate and Lower 10th Street, and turn right into Lower 9th Street. Pass The Point and bear left into Midsummer Place shopping centre. Cross the concourse and pass the police station. The Church of Christ the Cornerstone can be seen from here. Turn left towards Debenham's and Avebury Boulevard, turning right to the underpass. Walk down to Grafton Gate, veer right just before it and head for Midsummer Boulevard. Go through the underpasses and return to the railway station at the start.

Overleaf: The buildings at Bletchley Park (Walk 3)

15

Secrets of Bletchley Park

Puzzle over the enigma of Station X on this urban walk around Bletchley.

DISTANCE 6 miles (9.7km)	**MINIMUM TIME** 1hr 45min

ASCENT/GRADIENT Negligble ▲▲▲   **LEVEL OF DIFFICULTY** ✦✦✦

PATHS Roads, park and field paths, canal tow path and riverside walk, 2 stiles

LANDSCAPE Mixture of suburban streets and farmland

SUGGESTED MAP OS Explorer 192 Buckingham & Milton Keynes

START / FINISH Grid reference: SP 868337

DOG FRIENDLINESS Under control in Blue Lagoon Park, along Broad Walk and by canal. Dogs are permitted in grounds of Bletchley Park

PARKING Bletchley Station and approach road

PUBLIC TOILETS Bletchley Station and Bletchley Park

Bletchley Park. The name may sound ordinary enough but what took place here during the Second World War is quite remarkable. This was the home of Station X – where more than 10,000 people worked in total secrecy in a small, nondescript town at the heart of the English shires.

Brain Teasers

It was here that mathematicians, linguists, crossword enthusiasts and Oxbridge scholars battled for hours on end, in wooden huts and brick-built blocks, to break the seemingly unbreakable. Their role was to study the German military cipher machine, 'Enigma', and devise a programme to enable the Allies to decode the Nazis' secret radio messages. The odds against success were phenomenal, but they did succeed, shortening the war against Germany by as much as two years.

One of the key figures in the story of Bletchley Park was Alan Turing, a mathematical genius considered to be one of the pioneering fathers of the modern computer. It was he who invented the 'Bombe', an electro-mechanical machine of clattering code wheels intended to significantly reduce the time needed to break the daily-changing Enigma keys.

But why Bletchley Park? Midway between the universities of Oxford and Cambridge and just a few minutes' walk from a mainline railway station with regular services to London and many other parts of the country, it seemed a perfect venue for the Government Code and Cypher School. As the threat of war loomed, Bletchley Park was poised to become the key communications centre in the history of modern warfare.

In August 1939, code breakers arrived at Bletchley Park in large numbers. Their work had begun. They posed as members of 'Captain Ridley's shooting party' so as not to arouse suspicion in the area. Ridley was the man in charge of the school's move to Bletchley. For the next 40 years, no one outside Bletchley Park knew exactly what went on here, and the Germans never even realised Enigma had been broken.

WALK

3

WALK 3 DIRECTIONS

❶ From the station car park cross the road and to visit Bletchley Park turn right, its entrance now about 300yds (274m) further along Sherwood Drive. After the visit retrace your steps towards

the station and turn right on to the footpath opposite. This brings you into Wilton Road, the former entrance into Bletchley Park. Turn left along Wilton Avenue and left into Church Green Road. Bear left at the junction with Buckingham Road and head towards Central

Bletchley. Turn right into Water Eaton Road, pass beneath the Bletchley–Oxford rail line, and bear right at the footpath sign, just before the next railway bridge.

❷ Pass a pond, Pulmans Swannery, on the right and follow the fenced path to a stile. Continue to a fork, keep right and follow a track in an anti-clockwise direction round the edge of the lake. Avoid a ford and a footbridge and continue on the lakeside path. At the north-west corner of the lake, look for some steps and a footbridge on the right. Turn left immediately beyond them and follow a path parallel to power lines. Eventually bear left at a grassy track and follow it towards the railway line. Turn right immediately before a stile and keep to the right of the site of a house. Swing left at a fence to reach a stile, and then walk ahead with the railway line on your left.

❸ Pass through a tunnel of trees and alongside farmland eventually crossing a footbridge but always with the railway on your left and, when you reach the former drive to Slad Farm, exit to the road. Bear left, cross the railway bridge and turn immediately right at yellow posts. Follow the path for a short distance to a field corner and swing left to join a bridleway. Keep the houses of Bletchley on your left, beyond the trees and

hedgerow. On reaching the road, between two roundabouts, cross the canal bridge ahead and swing left to follow the Broad Walk. At a sign for the Riverside Walk, turn right and then swing left after about 75yds (69m).

❹ Keep the river a short distance away to the right. Draw level with a farm over to the right, cross a footbridge over a pond and turn left. Head for The Watermill and Mill Farm, avoiding the car park for Waterhall Park. Cross the bridge over the Grand Union Canal and keep right. Ahead now are several thatched and timber-framed cottages. Turn left in front of them and keep right at the main road junction, heading towards The Plough inn. Cross the road at the roundabout, following the sign for the station. Continue ahead through a residential area, pass beneath the two railway bridges seen near the start of the walk, go straight over at the junction and back to the station car park.

On to Magiovinium

A longer variation on Walk 3, passes the site of a Roman town.

See map and information panel for Walk 3

DISTANCE *7 miles (11.3km)*   **MINIMUM TIME** *2hr 45min*

ASCENT/GRADIENT *Negligble* ▲▲▲   **LEVEL OF DIFFICULTY** ✦✦✦

WALK 4 DIRECTIONS
(Walk 3 option)

At Point **A**, with Waterhall Park on your right, join the tow path of the Grand Union Canal and follow it north towards Fenny Stratford. Pass a milepost 'Braunston 39 miles'. Head for the bridge and keep ahead, with the tower of Fenny Stratford church in view among the rooftops on the opposite bank.

The land over to the right was once part of the Roman town of Magiovinium. The bank and ditch surrounding it can be identified in aerial photographs and the site is protected as a scheduled ancient monument. The enclosed part of Magiovinium straddles Watling Street and covered about 18.5 acres (7.5ha). The interior layout of the town, which was unwalled, would have comprised a grid pattern of streets along similar lines to neighbouring Milton Keynes.

Head towards a lift bridge and a private marina. Leave the tow path just beyond it, turn left at the road, cross the canal bridge, and pass the Bridge Inn, The Entertainers and the Swan Hotel. Bear left into Aylesbury Street, signposted 'Central Bletchley and Water Eaton'. Pass the church on the corner and walk along to The Maltsters and The Bull and Butcher. Continue to the mini-roundabout and turn right into Vicarage Road, Point **B**.

Bletchley and Fenny Stratford are like period pieces and many of the Victorian and Edwardian houses in these streets have changed little since the Second World War when large numbers of the code breakers working at nearby Bletchley Park were billeted here. Most spare rooms were let at that time.

Pass Browne Willis Close and Queensway Methodist church and follow the road to Knowles Middle School, built in 1937. Adjacent to it is Knowles Nursery School. Further down on the right is the Bletchley Arms. Follow a pedestriansed street, Elizabeth Square, and keep ahead at the next road, between shops. Pass the Conservative Club on the right and, when the road bends right, go forward towards the Brunel shopping centre. Pass alongside Boots and go left up a ramp to Brunel Roundabout and pass the Park pub on the left. Pass beneath the railway line, turn right at the police station into Sherwood Drive and return to the station.

Trailing Around Addington

Follow field paths to the heart of the countryside, part of a unique network of rights of way throughout England and Wales.

DISTANCE 4.25 miles (6.8km) **MINIMUM TIME** 1hr 45min

ASCENT/GRADIENT 88ft (27m) ▲▲▲ **LEVEL OF DIFFICULTY** +++

PATHS Quiet country road, stretches of field paths, North Buckinghamshire Way and Cross Bucks Way, 17 stiles

LANDSCAPE Gently undulating farmland either side of Claydon Brook

SUGGESTED MAP OS Explorer 192 Buckingham & Milton Keynes

START / FINISH Grid reference: SP 742285

DOG FRIENDLINESS On lead on road and near livestock

PARKING Limited space by church in Addington

PUBLIC TOILETS None en route

WALK 5 DIRECTIONS

In recent years the simple activity of walking has become one of Britain's most popular outdoor pastimes, With 140,000 miles (225,260km) of rights of way in England and Wales alone, it's hardly surprising that people spend so much of their leisure time eagerly exploring the hills and dales, woods and moorland to be found in this glorious countryside.

Some footpaths came into being as vital trade routes or packhorse trails, while others were drove roads established to convey sheep and cattle. Pilgrim tracks and green lanes steered medieval wayfarers between the great centres of Christianity, Winchester and Canterbury. In the 18th and 19th centuries the agricultural revolution and Enclosure Acts were responsible for major changes in the countryside, producing a vastly different, almost unrecognisable landscape and introducing a host of new paths and tracks.

Over recent years many long distance trails have appeared on Britain's rights of way map. These range from 10 miles (16.1km) to over 300 miles (483km) and reflect the best of our varied countryside and ever-changing scenery. Two of Buckinghamshire's more popular trails meet on this walk, providing ramblers with the opportunity to explore the rural heart of the county. The Cross Bucks Way runs across Buckinghamshire for 24 miles (39km) from the Oxfordshire border to the Grand Union Canal near Leighton Buzzard, while the North Buckinghamshire Way is 30 miles (48km) long and extends from Chequers to Milton Keynes.

WHERE TO EAT AND DRINK

The Verney Arms at Verney Junction welcomes walkers and offers an imaginative menu. Typical lunch dishes include pie of the day, steak sandwich and shepherds pie.

ADDINGTON

Keep Addington Church on your right and an executive house with a well in the front garden on your left and, through the gate, follow the North Bucks Way out of Addington, across farmland. Make for a stile and footbridge over the Claydon Brook. Continue ahead to a stile and plank bridge and keep to the right edge of the next field. Over to the left lies Furzen Farm. Cross a track and a stile, then make for a kissing gate leading out to a disused railway. A 'stop, look and listen' sign is still in place. Follow the North Bucks Way, keeping the old 1870 station buildings on the right.

The canopied entrance is a reminder of the days when Verney Junction was a working station. Look out, too, for the Victorian postbox. Walk along the road to the Verney Arms and keep right at the junction. Follow the road past Littleworth Farm and bear right at the next junction for Buckingham and Padbury. Re-cross the old railway at the next bridge and continue along the road, following it round a left bend. Turn right just before Claydon Hill Farm and join the Cross Bucks Way. Cross a stile and bridge and follow the fence along to a second stile.

Go diagonally right in the next field, passing under electricity cables, and cross a dismantled railway via two stiles. Go straight ahead in the next field to a galvanised gate and then, through the gate, veer to the left of a stand of trees. Look for a stile and a footbridge with a stile at each end and, across them, veer diagonally right. Across the field are two gates; make for the left-hand one and head diagonally up the field, towards the top right corner. Draw level with Hill Farm, pass through a gate, cross a track and a stile, then go half left to reach a track and three stiles. Over these, aim diagonally right across the field to a stile and galvanised gate and go straight ahead into the next field through a gate and head to a stile, footbridge and waymark. Don't cross over, but perform a 150 degree turn and head for two stiles in the boundary hedge, in line with a gabled former schoolhouse.

Head diagonally right towards the houses of Addington and make for a stile by a lane. Bear left and walk along the lane to a road junction with a traffic arrow. Turn right here, then bear right again at the next junction and return to the church.

Claydon's Lady with the Lamp

Visit a splendid National Trust house and see the bedroom occupied by Florence Nightingale on this walk around the Claydon villages.

DISTANCE 5.5miles (8.8km)	MINIMUM TIME 2hrs
ASCENT/GRADIENT 160ft (49m) ▲▲▲	LEVEL OF DIFFICULTY +++

PATHS Field paths and tracks, several stretches of road, 4 stiles

LANDSCAPE Gentle farmland and parkland in the Vale of Aylesbury

SUGGESTED MAP OS Explorer 192 Buckingham & Milton Keynes

START/FINISH Grid reference: SP 739255

DOG FRIENDLINESS Dogs on lead at all times, some fields with livestock

PARKING On-street parking in road leading to St Mary the Virgin Church, East Claydon

PUBLIC TOILETS Claydon House

Standing amid elegant parkland, studded with cedar, oak, horse chestnut, holm oak and Wellingtonia trees, is 18th-century Claydon House, replacing an earlier building and now in the care of the National Trust. Only one third of the house remains and, seeing it for the first time, you may be struck by its simplicity, yet it presents to the visitor a series of magnificent and distinctive rococo state rooms with carving by Luke Lightfoot. Also on view is the bedroom used by Florence Nightingale (1820–1910) during her visits to her sister who lived here.

Claydon House

In 1620 Edmund Verney, Knight-Marshal and Standard Bearer to Charles I, became the first Verney to occupy Claydon. Later, during the 18th century, the family succeeded to an earldom and Edmund's great great grandson, Ralph, 2nd Earl Verney, began to remodel the Tudor manor house, attempting to outdo nearby Stowe (see Walk 1). This work still forms the core of the three-storey brick east wing, although the design has disappeared as a result of successive rebuilding. Ralph also added the stone-faced west wing, employing the services of the unknown Luke Lightfoot, an eccentric and enigmatic figure who had acquired certain skills as a craftsman and was variously described as a cabinetmaker, carver, architect and surveyor.

Penniless and Miserable

However, there was a darker side to Lightfoot. He was also a swindler, which almost certainly came to light just as his work was nearing completion, as he was dismissed in 1769. Undeterred, Verney continued with his building plan, though now beset by financial problems. He added a domed entrance hall to the west wing and beyond that a ballroom, but died soon after in 1791, penniless and miserable. His niece, Lady Fermanagh, inherited Claydon and within a year she had demolished her uncle's precious ballroom and entrance hall. The house was bequeathed by the Verney family to the National Trust in 1956.

THE CLAYDONS

The Lady With the Lamp

Florence Nightingale, whose sister married Sir Harry Verney, was a frequent visitor to Claydon between the late 1850s and 1895. She would often spend her summers at the house and over the fireplace in her bedroom is a portrait of the *Lady with the Lamp* by W B Richmond. Adjacent to it is a watercolour by Chalon depicting Florence, her sister and their mother. A museum displays Verney family mementoes and objects associated with Florenence Nightingale and her experiences during the Crimean War.

WALK 6 DIRECTIONS

❶ Walk along Church Way and continue ahead in the village centre. Keep right at the next junction, following Sandhill Road. Pass a row of houses set back from the road and swing left just before a brick and timber cottage to pass through a galvanised gate. Go straight ahead towards the next gate and look for a gate and waymark a few paces to the left of it. Through it, keep ahead in the field, with the boundary on your right. Make for a gate in the corner and cross the field to the boundary. Continue ahead with the hedgerow on the left and follow a track along the field perimeter, heading for the buildings of Home Farm. Look for

25

a plank bridge and kissing gate to the left of the track and cross the cemetery to a stile by the road.

② Bear left and follow the road for 600yds (549m), passing the entrance to Home Farm on the right and a footpath on the left. Turn left and follow the drive to Claydon House and nearing the house, bear right at a waymark post through two gates and turn left. Keep Claydon House and the church on your left and continue alongside the ha-ha, with the lake over to your right. Cut through the parkland to a gate, merge with the drive to Claydon House and follow it to the road.

WHERE TO EAT AND DRINK

There are no pubs on the route of the walk. However, nearby Winslow and Buckingham offer a good choice of inns, cafés and restaurants. Refreshments are also available at Claydon House.

③ Turn right and pass a lay-by. Continue along the roadside until you reach a stile in the left boundary. Head diagonally left towards a hedge corner and then, maintaining the same direction, make for the extreme left corner of Home Wood, cross a stile into the next field. Walk half left, the woodland edge on your right, passing left of a small pond, to a gap in the hedge with a waymark post and a plank bridge. Make for

WHILE YOU'RE THERE

If time allows, leave the route of the walk near Claydon House and explore the local countryside on permissive paths. The routes are part of what is known as the Conservation Walks Project, which is funded by companies under the Landfill Tax Credit Scheme. Open permitted access allows walkers to enjoy Claydon's parkland and walk round the lakes to the west of the house.

a gate and stile ahead and cross a tarmac drive to Muxwell Farm.

④ Beyond a gate, head diagonally left and look for a waymark in the line of trees across the pasture. Veer right in the next field, making for a stile and post in the boundary. Walk diagonally right across the field to the far corner, pass through a gap and keep to the right edge of the pasture. Bear right at a gateway to a track and turn left. Walk along to the road and turn right.

⑤ Walk through Botolph Claydon and bear left at the junction, following the signs for East Claydon and Winslow. Pass Botolph Farmhouse, the village library and hall and the thatched seat built round a tree. Follow the pavement to a sign 'footpath only, no horses'. Take the path back to East Claydon.

WHAT TO LOOK OUT FOR

St Mary the Virgin Church at East Claydon is tucked away on the edge of the village. Its record of presiding rectors dates back to 1218. The tower was built in the late 15th century, while the chapel was added to the nave in 1230. Over the years the local villages have united to become the parish of the Claydons. Look out for the former library at Botolph Claydon, built in 1900 and now the village hall. Adjacent to it is a clock tower erected in 1913 by the friends and parishioners of Sir Edmund Verney in remembrance of his work for the welfare of the parish and his gift of the hall and library.

Mentmore and the Crime of the Century

A pleasant amble in the Vale of Aylesbury, passing the site of the 20th century's most audacious crime.

DISTANCE 6.5 miles (10.4km)		**MINIMUM TIME** 2hrs 45min	
ASCENT/GRADIENT 180ft (55m) ▲▲▲		**LEVEL OF DIFFICULTY** +++	

PATHS Field paths and tracks, roads and canal tow path, 2 stiles

LANDSCAPE Vale of Aylesbury and farmland west of Grand Union Canal

SUGGESTED MAP OS Explorers 181 Chiltern Hills North; 192 Milton Keynes & Buckingham

START/FINISH Grid reference: SP 907196 (on Explorer 181)

DOG FRIENDLINESS On lead across farmland and under control on tow path

PARKING Limited parking in vicinity of The Stag pub at Mentmore

PUBLIC TOILETS None en route

It hardly seems possible today, but in the summer of 1963, 15 masked men waited in the darkness of the Buckinghamshire countryside, held up the night train from Glasgow to London and robbed it of £2.5 million It was described as the crime of the century, making newspaper headlines around the world and eventually turning the robbers into folk heroes, immortalised in books, television series and money-spinning movies. The robbers were pursued and captured by Scotland Yard and many of them were given long prison sentences. But the story did not end there. One of them, Ronald Biggs, broke out of jail, fled to Brazil and eluded capture for the next 35 years.

These days, surplus and used bank notes are transported around the country in security vans, but in the very different world of the early 1960s, express trains conveyed such consignments – often with huge amounts of money on board. And 40 years ago it was possible to stop a mail train and rob it – as was proved.

The men planned the snatch in meticulous detail, surveying the railway line between London and Rugby in an attempt to find an isolated stretch of track with a signal and easy access to the road. Eventually they found what they were looking for – Sears Crossing and nearby Bridego Bridge on the Buckinghamshire/Bedfordshire border, to the south of Leighton Buzzard. They made many trips here in the dead of night, to identify the mail trains and plan the job.

Satisfied that it could be done, the next step was to familiarise themselves with the technicalities of train engines and braking systems. To do this, they dressed up in navy blue boiler suits, passing themselves off as railway workers in the marshalling yards of London's mainline stations. In the early hours of Thursday 8 August, 1963, the men were as ready as they ever would be. It was time to go.

Travelling in a convoy of vehicles, they made their way across country to the four-track railway. Their first task was to cut the telephone wires to the nearby farms. Then, as the mail train approached, they covered the

27

green light with a glove and used a battery and a bulb behind the red signal to give the impression to the driver that the light was against him.

The train stopped, but the driver refused to co-operate and received violent blows to the head. With the engine and the vital post office coaches detached from the rest of the train, the men moved the express down the line to Bridego Bridge where they unloaded 120 sacks on to the vehicles lined up on the road below. They drove off as dawn gradually lit the scene of their extraordinary crime. (See Walk 11 to find out what happened next.)

WALK 7 DIRECTIONS

❶ Walk back to the junction by The Stag, turn right and pass one of the grand entrances to Mentmore Towers. Follow the road round to the left, then to the right by the Church of St Mary the Virgin. Continue along the road and bear right at a stile,

just beyond Old Vicarage Cottage. Go down the field, keeping the fence over to the right, and look for a stile in the bottom boundary to the left of a solitary oak and farm sheds.

❷ Over the stile veer right for 50 paces to a plank bridge, then swing left to skirt the field,

WHERE TO EAT AND DRINK

The Stag at Mentmore offers a varied menu in the bar, with dishes such as grilled chicken in sesame bread, open sandwiches with black pudding, poached egg and bacon, and smoked haddock with Welsh rarebit. There is also a restaurant and à la carte menu.

4 Bear right at the sign for Grove Church and Farm and walk down to the Grand Union Canal at Church Lock. Pass Church Lock Cottage before turning right to join the tow path. Follow it for about 1 mile (1.6km) and, 140yds (128m) before a bridge, where you can see a weir on the left, leave the tow path at a plank bridge and bear right for 40 paces to the field corner.

keeping a ditch on the left. On reaching the next plank bridge and waymark, look for a pond enclosed by fencing. Follow the path alongside it and then through a young copse into the next field. Pass under telegraph wires to the next plank bridge in the boundary. Go ahead into a large field and pass under electricity cables. The houses of Ledburn can be seen ahead. Make for a footbridge and in the next field, where the ditch veers sharply right, go ahead and aim slightly left, towards a house with a white-painted gable. Keep to the left of it and turn right at the road.

5 Swing left and keep the boundary on your right. Make for two metal gates leading out to the road, turn right then left at the turning for Wing and Ledburn. Follow the road to Bridego Bridge, pass beneath the railway and keep ahead to Rowden Farm.

6 Bear left at the T-junction for Mentmore. Pass Mentmore Courts, Howell Hill Close and The Stud House before turning left at the end of a stretch of pavement. Opposite the junction are two wooden gates leading into a field. Follow the road round to the right and return to the playground and parking area.

WHAT TO LOOK OUT FOR

The former Church of St Michael and All Angels by Church Lock was once the smallest church in the county and is mentioned in the Domesday Book. The church was rebuilt during the 14th century and declared redundant in 1971. It is now a private house.

3 Go through Ledburn and make for a left bend. On the left is Cornfield Cottage, once a chapel. Cross the road to a kissing gate and follow a track running across farmland. As it curves left, keep ahead, following the path across a field. At a track, turn right and follow it to Sears Crossing. Cross the railway bridge, follow the track down to the road and turn left.

WHILE YOU'RE THERE

Have a look at the Church of St Mary the Virgin at Mentmore. According to records, there was a church on this site in the 12th century, probably consisting of a chancel and nave. Make for the wooded corner of the churchyard and you'll get a glimpse of splendid Mentmore Towers, once the home of Lord Rosebery, British Liberal Prime Minister in the latter years of the 19th century. The house, overlooking elegant parkland, remained in the Rosebery family for many years, but has since been owned by the late George Harrison who donated it to the Natural Law Party.

Making Tracks at Quainton

*Recall the great days of steam travel on this
walk to Waddesdon.*

DISTANCE 5 miles (8km)	MINIMUM TIME 2hrs
ASCENT/GRADIENT Negligible ▲▲▲	LEVEL OF DIFFICULTY ✦✦✦

PATHS Mainly field paths, some stretches of road, parts of
North Buckinghamshire Way and Midshires Way, 21 stiles

LANDSCAPE Gentle farmland in Vale of Aylesbury

SUGGESTED MAP OS Explorer 181 Chiltern Hills North

START/FINISH Grid reference: SP 736189

DOG FRIENDLINESS Mostly on lead, particularly near farm buildings

PARKING Brill Tramway Path car park, parking on extreme left.
Permission given by Buckinghamshire Railway Centre

PUBLIC TOILETS Buckinghamshire Railway Centre

The Buckinghamshire Railway Centre is one of those wonderful visitor attractions where, if you've the spirit and the imagination, you can wallow for hours in nostalgia, reliving the days when Britain could be justly proud of its railway system.

Covering 25 acres (10ha), the site hosts one of the country's largest independent collections of railway engines and rolling stock, with vintage steam train rides and half-day steam locomotive driving courses among its attractions. As you begin your tour of the centre, gazing in awe at the Victorian station with its flower-filled platform and nostalgic adverts, and the steam engines, the leviathans of the railway age, being restored in the nearby sheds, spare a moment to consider how it all began.

In 1968 the London Railway Preservation Society decided on Quainton Road Station to store old railway stock and memorabilia, leading to the birth of a new railway visitor attraction. It chose the meeting point of three railways – the Metropolitan Railway, the Brill Tramway and the London extension of the Great Central Railway. The London Railway Preservation Society became the Quainton Railway Society Ltd whose dedicated members now own and operate the Buckinghamshire Railway Centre.

Opened in 1868 as part of the Aylesbury and Buckingham Railway, Quainton Road Station was absorbed by the Metropolitan Railway in 1890, becoming one of those far-flung rural stations you tend to associate with the best of Ealing comedy films. In those days you could change at Quainton Road for the Metropolitan Line and travel all the way to Baker Street. Look out for the authentic station sign on the platform at Quainton Road, advising passengers to change here for the Metropolitan Line. By the turn of the 19th century, it was also possible to travel from here direct to London's Marylebone or north to Manchester.

The Beeching cuts of the 1960s sounded the line's death knell. In 1963 the station closed to passenger traffic and three years later the Great Central main line closed and the line through the station was a single track.

0 ½ mile
0 ½ km

Quainton

North Buckinghamshire Way

1 P

Railway Centre

Quainton Road Station

82 ▲

—N—

92 ▲

5

3

Littleton Manor Farm

Glebe Farm

A41

← Bicester

Waddesdon

The Bell PH

The Lion PH

→ Aylesbury

A41

The Five Arrows PH

4

C

159 ▲ Lodge Hill

Waddesdon Manor

A

Wormstone

B

Windmill Manor

WALK 8 DIRECTIONS

❶ Leave the car park, turn left and cross the road bridge over the railway. From the bridge there is a good view of the railway centre and the preserved station. The entrance to the site is on the right. On leaving the railway centre, bear right and follow Station Road towards Quainton. Pass lines of houses and, when the road curves round to the left by a bus stop, turn right at a footpath sign and stile to follow a track between fields. Quainton and its windmill can be seen over to the left. Go through a gateway and turn right to join the North Buckinghamshire Way.

❷ Follow the edge of the field to a kissing gate by a field gate and continue to a stile in the distant boundary. Over the stile continue ahead and, passing through two sets of steel field gates, cross three stiles and a footbridge. Cross a small field, then a stile to cross the railway line, Quainton Road Station lies away to your right. Cross two stiles and, through a hedge, follow path along the field margin to a stile, by electricity poles and a metal crash barrier. The outline of Waddesdon Manor can now be glimpsed up in the trees, to the right of the church. Over the stile continue straight ahead on a concrete farm track and where the track bends right, cross a stile into the field and turn immediately right.

❸ Skirt Glebe Farm and cross a track via two stiles, continuing on the North Buckinghamshire Way. Aim diagonally right to two stiles and continue alongside a hedgerow in the next field. Cross two stiles and join an enclosed path running into Waddesdon. On reaching the A41, turn right, crossing Quainton Road and Frederick Street. Pass the Lion, the Methodist church and the post office before reaching the parish church of St Michael and All Angels on the right.

❹ Follow the road out of the village, passing The Bell pub. Keep to the A41 and look for an old cast-iron milepost, 'London 44 miles'. In 50yds (46m), beyond the speed derestriction sign, turn right at a stile and waymark. Cut through the trees to a second stile and continue ahead in the field. Cross a concrete farm track, pass under power lines and aim for a stile and footbridge in the boundary hedge. Littleton Manor Farm can be seen near by.

❺ Aim slightly left in the next field to reach a stile and then go diagonally left across the next pasture to a stile in the far corner. Over the stile continue alongside left-hand hedge and make for two stiles, by gates turn right and follow the road or footpath parallel to the road and between hedges back to the car park.

Waddesdon Five Arrows

An extra loop through parkland, glimpsing a sumptuous château.

See map and information panel for Walk 8

DISTANCE *3 miles (4.8km)*   **MINIMUM TIME** *1hr 15min*

ASCENT/GRADIENT *250ft (76m)* ▲▲▲   **LEVEL OF DIFFICULTY** +++

WALK 9 DIRECTIONS
(Walk 8 option)

Mayer Amschel Rothschild founded the banking dynasty in Frankfurt in the 18th century. The family coat of arms focuses on a red shield and includes a fist holding five arrows. The arrows represent his five sons, four of whom established banking houses in Europe's other financial centres – London, Vienna, Naples and Paris. Close family ties between the branches were maintained over the years. Several of the houses in Waddesdon, including the village hall, were rebuilt by Ferdinand de Rothschild and can be distinguished by maroon-painted gables and other architectural detail. Look out for the five arrows seen on various buildings during this walk.

Before Point **4** on Walk 8, just beyond The Five Arrows pub, turn left by the war memorial. Avoid the path on the right and head for the public entrance to Waddesdon Manor, a French Renaissance-style château built by Ferdinand de Rothschild in the late 19th century. Through the ornate gates follow the drive through trees and where it veers left go straight on along a grass track, the cricket ground on your right, to a T-junction, Point **A**. Go straight on uphill, past the sign for Windmill Hill Farm. Continue on the bridleway as it bends right and left crossing two cattle grids. At the farm buildings, follow the track left and then immediately right, passing a pair of cottages on the left. Descend the slope to a gate and, through the gate, turn right. Skirt the field, make for a ditch in the corner and continue ahead. Head for the next boundary, go through the gates and turn right through a kissing gate, Point **B**.

Walk ahead, keeping to the field boundary, and head for a kissing gate in the corner. Continue along the field-edge to a kissing gate on the right. Cross a footbridge and stile, then turn half left in the adjacent field and head for a gap in the trees. Go up the slope to a broad drive, veer right and pass a waymark as you emerge from the woodland. Branch half left at the next waymark, Point **C**, and take the grassy path across the slopes.

Head for a kissing gate to the right of three tall Wellingtonias and follow the path across pasture, towards woodland. Head for a kissing gate, pick your way through the trees to a drive and cross over towards Waddesdon. Pass garages and a house with the five arrows emblem before returning to the war memorial at Point **4** on Walk 8.

Topping Ivinghoe Beacon

Climb to a lofty viewpoint before following Britain's oldest road.

DISTANCE 4 miles (6.4km)	**MINIMUM TIME** 1hr 45min

ASCENT/GRADIENT 280ft (85m) ▲▲▲   **LEVEL OF DIFFICULTY** +++

PATHS Farmland and woodland paths, some road walking, 3 stiles

LANDSCAPE Mix of remote farmland and typical Chiltern scenery

SUGGESTED MAP OS Explorer 181 Chiltern Hills North

START / FINISH Grid reference: SP 963159

DOG FRIENDLINESS On lead across initial farmland and under control on Icknield Way and Ridgeway

PARKING Official car park near Ivinghoe Beacon

PUBLIC TOILETS None en route

WALK 10 DIRECTIONS

Ivinghoe Beacon is a suitably dramatic setting for the start of the Ridgeway. You can picture this ancient trade route as it once was, busy with travellers. Cattle drovers used it regularly, as did locals on short journeys, long distance traders and pilgrims.

Leave the car park for the road and keep left. Pass a track on the left and cross a cattle grid. Continue through woodland to a field gate and footpath sign on the left. Skirt the field, with trees on the left, to a stile. Veer half left in the next field, keeping to the

WHERE TO EAT AND DRINK

There are no pubs on the route of the walk, but many of the surrounding towns and villages offer a good choice of food and drink. Try The Stag at Mentmore (see Walk 7), the historic Greyhound coaching inn at Aldbury or one of the waterside pubs at Marsworth near Tring.

left of Ward's Hurst Farm. Cross a stile, look for a waymark by the outbuildings, bear left, then go through a gate and keep the fence on your right. Pass under power lines to a kissing gate and take the Icknield Way through the Ashridge Estate.

Follow the waymarked trail, including a steep descent of steps, through woodland to a kissing gate and continue ahead, still on the Icknield Way, avoiding the Boundary Trail branching off to the right. Through kissing gate keep the fence on your left, climbing gently via two kissing gates to a marker stone for the Icknield Way, the Peddars Way and the Ridgeway. Turn sharp right to a kissing gate and gate and follow a clear track striking out across expansive downland. By a fence corner, head up the steep slope to the ridge and bear left along it to a kissing gate. This stretch of the walk offers grand views of Ivinghoe Beacon and the surrounding countryside. Walk ahead along the ridge at the

IVINGHOE BEACON

Ridgeway sign, making for the start of the National Trail.

The Ridgeway extends for 85 miles (137km) through the Buckinghamshire Chilterns to the Thames and then across Berkshire into Wiltshire. In places the trail is as wide as a main road or a dual carriageway. When the original line became weathered or difficult to negotiate, travellers moved from one side to the other, gradually making the track wider.

The character of the Ridgeway changes the further west you travel. Initially, the trail cuts through beech wood scenery, glorious in autumn, and across soft rolling hills. Over the Thames, the landscape assumes a totally different character. From the river onwards, the Ridgeway cuts across bleak, exposed downland, offering little in the way of shelter on a wet or windy day. This stretch of the Ridgeway explores a landscape littered with long barrows, prehistoric forts and monuments.

The downs of Berkshire and Wiltshire and the softer country of the Chilterns are remnants of a landscape of huge domes and ridges formed around 25 million years ago. The upper strata consists of great ridges of chalk laid down in the sea probably more than 60 million years ago.

Whether you are interested in history or geology, a walk along the Ridgeway is a journey through time. Here you can walk for miles without seeing another soul, following in the footsteps of 300 generations and seeing the same tracts of chalk downland, the same distant hills and the same broad river. Today, walkers can follow the route from start to finish, but that hasn't always been the case. In 1942 the Ramblers Association proposed a long distance route across this part of southern England, but it was another 30 years before it was officially opened to the public. With its access to villages and overnight accommodation, many people choose the Ridgeway for a very pleasant walking holiday, allowing up to a week to complete the route at a leisurely pace.

With your back to the Ridgeway plinth, follow the trail as it runs south. Descend steeply, keep left at the fork and make for the road. Cross over and continue on the National Trail, beginning a moderate climb. Go through a kissing gate and cut between trees before spotting a deep combe cutting in to the hillside on the right. Pass two stiles by gates and when the Ridgeway sweeps right by a waymark, bear left and head up the steep slope to a stile. Cross a track just beyond it and follow the woodland footpath until you reach the drive to Clipper Down Cottage. Join the road here, turn left and return to the car park.

Brill and a Farmhouse Den of Thieves

Enjoy good views across Buckinghamshire on this breezy walk beginning in a sprawling hilltop village.

DISTANCE *4 miles (6.4km)* MINIMUM TIME *1hr 30min*

ASCENT/GRADIENT *350ft (107m)* ▲▲▲ LEVEL OF DIFFICULTY +++

PATHS *Field paths and tracks, several stretches of road, 9 stiles*

LANDSCAPE *Mixture of farmland and rolling country*

SUGGESTED MAP *OS Explorer 180 Oxford, Witney & Woodstock*

START/FINISH *Grid reference: SP 653141*

DOG FRIENDLINESS *On lead across farmland where there might be cattle*

PARKING *Room to park by windmill*

PUBLIC TOILETS *None en route*

After successfully holding up the night mail train from Glasgow to London in the early hours of Thursday 8 August, 1963 (see Walk 7), the Great Train Robbers journeyed 27 or so miles (43.5km) west, across country to a farm near the village of Brill. This was to be their hideout, where they could lay low for a day or two after the robbery.

Remote Hideaway

Leatherslade Farm was just what they wanted – remotely situated on high ground and well away from the road. The men chose the site in the same way that the Romans and the people of the Iron Age chose their hilltop settlements – so they could spot any sign of an approaching enemy. Initially they considered using a fleet of high-powered 3.8 litre engined Jaguars as getaway cars. That way they could be back in London in an hour. But driving at high speed through Buckinghamshire's country lanes in the middle of the night was perhaps not the wisest option.

After careful consideration, they hit upon the idea of looking for a suitable hideout within half an hour's drive of the bridge. In June the men spotted a farm advertised in the local press and after viewing it, made an offer of £5,550, which was accepted. The owners moved out at the end of July and a week later, on the morning of Tuesday 6 August, members of the gang began to arrive at the farm. By midnight the following evening they were ready for action.

A Clean Sweep

They returned to Leatherslade Farm after the train robbery and began digging a hole in the garden to bury the mailbags. They cleaned the farm from top to bottom, wiping down the surfaces and burning all the shoes and clothes that had been worn during the raid. Using several vans to carry the money, the gang eventually left the farm late on the Friday night – nearly 48 hours after the robbery.

The following Monday, a local farm labourer walked up the track to Leatherslade Farm to look at some of his cows. He noticed that the windows had been blacked out. Climbing through the hedge into the yard, he spotted a five-ton army truck in the shed. Somewhat suspicious, he rang the police who were busy taking up to 400 train robbery-related calls a day. Eventually they arrived at the farm and discovered the lorry, two Land Rovers, a half-dug hole and the remains of a bonfire.

Both inside the farm and out the police found numerous clues indicating that this had been the Great Train Robbers hideout. But they needed proof and the gang had removed any incriminating evidence that could link them to the farm – or so they thought. Ronald Biggs had left his prints on a tomato sauce bottle in the kitchen. It was just what the police had been looking for.

WALK 11 DIRECTIONS

❶ From the car park go down the lane known as South Hills, beside The Pheasant Inn, keeping the windmill visible on your right. At a private lock-up garage and a waymark post, swing left to join a track. Follow as it curves round to the right to a pair of garages and enter an enclosed footpath to their right. A pretty cottage can be seen on the right. Keep to the enclosed footpath and head over three stiles before crossing rolling grassland. Head towards a large house and a stile to the left of it. Cross over to the road and turn right.

2 Pass a public footpath sign, then look for a bridleway and footpath sign further down on the right, go 50 paces along the track then left over a stile and cross into the field. Head diagonally right over the brow and down the field to a plank bridge and stile. Aim broadly left down the adjoining field, making for a stile just to the right of a white cottage with four dormer windows. Turn left and follow a footpath towards the cottage. Keep left and bear right after a few paces on to the lane into Oakley. Walk along Little London Green to the road and turn right.

WHAT TO LOOK OUT FOR

Almost at the end of the walk, just beyond the turning to Oakley, is a rarely seen barometer in the wall, dating back to 1910. The barometer was erected in memory of Sir Edmund Verney of Claydon House (see Walk 6) in grateful recognition of his devotion to the welfare of the people of Brill and district as county councillor.

3 Take the first path on the left, opposite Little London Farm. Over a stile head diagonally left in the field, pass under power lines and make for the right hand of two steel field gates. Through this gate cross the next field to a waymark and galvanised field gate and then continue ahead across the next pasture to a stile and track. Bear left and walk up the track towards Leatherslade Farm. As you approach the farm gate, take the bridle path to the left of it and skirt the house and outbuildings. This is a modern house, built to replace the original

WHERE TO EAT AND DRINK

There are a couple of pubs in Brill – The Red Lion and The Pheasant, which is conveniently situated at the walk's start/finish.

farmhouse used by the gang during the robbery.

4 Once clear of the farmhouse buildings, the green lane bears left and keeps climbing gently, passing a public footpath on the right. At the end of the green lane go through a galvanised gate. Continue ahead, with the field boundary on your right. Pass several more footpaths on the right and keep going until you reach a field gate in the top boundary. Follow the track ahead to the road by the entrance to a house.

5 Keep left here and walk along the road to Brill. Pass the Wesleyan chapel, over to the right across the green is the village church. The Red Lion can also be seen at this end of Brill. Pass a turning on the left to Oakley and look for the barometer in the wall. Bear left into Windmill Street and return to the car park.

WHILE YOU'RE THERE

Before starting the walk, take a close look at Brill Windmill standing on the edge of the village. The present mill dates from around 1680 and is actually a post mill – a windmill whose whole body revolves around a central post to face the wind. One of the oldest post mills, with Pitstone Windmill seen on Walk 10 and perhaps the oldest of all, in the country, Brill was last used in 1919 for milling barley. The nearby pits indicate that clay was extracted for use in brick and tile manufacture.

Hartwell's Green Abode

Combine the pleasure of a walk beside the River Thame with a stroll through the grounds of a hotel with a remarkable history.

DISTANCE 5 miles (8km)	**MINIMUM TIME** 2hrs
ASCENT/GRADIENT 180ft (55m) ▲▲▲	**LEVEL OF DIFFICULTY** +++
PATHS Field and riverside paths, tracks and lanes, 7 stiles	
LANDSCAPE Gently rolling farmland and villages south of River Thame	
SUGGESTED MAP OS Explorer 181 Chiltern Hills North	
START/FINISH Grid reference: SP 783123	
DOG FRIENDLINESS On lead near Lower Hartwell Farm and alongside Thame	
PARKING Space in Eythrope Road, Hartwell	
PUBLIC TOILETS None en route	

*'Why wouldst thou leave
calm Hartwell's green abode…
Apician table and Horatian Ode?'*

So wrote Lord Byron on Louis XVIII's departure for France to assume his throne in 1814. Few hotels can boast such a royal connection, but it was in the library of Hartwell House, just outside Aylesbury, that its most famous resident, Louis XVIII, exiled King of France, signed the accession papers to the throne. Louis leased the house between 1809 and 1814, staying here with his court during the Napoleonic wars. The Queen of France died here during this period and her coffin was taken from Hartwell to Sardinia.

Good Old Boys

One of England's finest stately homes and grandest country hotels, Hartwell House was built for the Hampden and Lee families, ancestors of the American Civil War soldier, General Robert E Lee, during the 17th and 18th centuries. Now a Grade I listed building, the house has many Jacobean and Georgian features, magnificent decorative plasterwork, ceilings and panelling, fine paintings and antique furniture.

The philanthropist Ernest Edward Cook, grandson of tourism pioneer Thomas Cook, who was an important benefactor of the National Trust and National Art Collections Fund, bought Hartwell House and its estate from the Lees in 1938. He was also a founder of the Ernest Cook Trust, which, in the mid-1980s, made Hartwell House and its parkland available to Historic House Hotels for a major restoration and conversion.

Impressive Entrance

The entrance to the house is via a porch flanked by pillars of carved stone, and a carved doorway. Set above all this is a splendid oriel window sitting on intricately embroidered stone corbels. The great hall is an imposing room in English baroque style built by James Gibbs in 1740. The rococo morning room with its decorated ceiling and door cases, the adjoining drawing room and the library, are all Georgian and date from about 1760. The principal dining room of the 1980s is by Eric Throssell and reflects the style of the early 19th-century architect Sir John Soane. Hartwell stands in 90 acres (36ha) of parkland, which was laid out by a pupil of the eminent landscape designer Lancelot 'Capability' Brown. Among the features is a lake spanned by a delightful stone bridge and fed by nearby springs.

WALK 12 DIRECTIONS

❶ From the A418 turn into Bishopstone Road and keep to the left of the church. Through a kissing gate walk along to the footpath beside Manor Farm Close and cross the pasture to a kissing gate leading out to a recreation ground. Pass ornate gate pillars on the left, recalling the men of the village who died in the world wars, and exit to the road by railings. Cross over to a footpath sign and follow the drive to a timber garage and shed. Bear right and follow path to a gate and then follow the path to the road. Turn right, walk up to the A418 and on the right is the Rose and Crown.

❷ Swing left at the corner and follow the path alongside a stone wall. Head for the road, bear right and walk along to the entrance to Hartwell House. Veer left at the gate pillars and follow the waymarked path through the hotel grounds. Go through a kissing gate, keep the church on your right and the little graveyard on your left. Turn right at the road and pass the Egyptian Well. Avoid the North Bucks Way running off to the left, pass Lower Hartwell Farm and turn left at the footpath. Cross two fields via three stiles and turn right immediately beyond a plank bridge.

❸ Skirt the field and make for a stile ahead. Keep the hedge on your left and continue on the North Bucks Way, heading towards Waddon Hill Farm. Cross a stile, walk ahead alongside timber barns and turn left at the waymark. Follow the track out across the fields, keeping alongside a hedge, to where it eventually it sweeps left. Leave it at this point and go straight on along a path to a stile. Cross a meadow and head for the River Thame. Swing left at the river bank to a gate and join the Thame Valley Walk.

❹ After about 100yds (91m) the path reaches a second gate at the point where the river begins a wide loop away to the right. Follow the stream to the next gate and rejoin the river bank. Follow the Thame, avoiding the bridleway branching away from the river, and continue on the waymarked trail. Via a kissing gate, make for a footbridge, then another at a weir. On the opposite bank is an ornate lodge. Join a straight concrete track via a stile and follow it towards trees.

❺ Once in the trees, the Thame can be seen immediately on the left. To the right is the parkland of Eythrope. Bear right at the next junction to glimpse the park. To continue the walk, turn left through gates, keep left and follow the tarmac drive. Begin a moderate lengthy ascent, eventually passing through gates at the crest, before reaching the houses of Stone.

Chequers – Country Seat of our Chosen Leaders

Explore the rolling Chilterns and savour glimpses of a famous Elizabethan mansion – rural retreat of the Prime Minister.

WALK 13

DISTANCE 5 miles (8km)   **MINIMUM TIME** 2hrs

ASCENT/GRADIENT 378ft (115m) ▲▲▲   **LEVEL OF DIFFICULTY** ✚✚✚

PATHS Field and woodland paths and tracks, stretch of Ridgeway, 8 stiles

LANDSCAPE Chiltern country, a mixture of rolling hills and woodland

SUGGESTED MAP OS Explorer 181 Chiltern Hills North

START/FINISH Grid reference: SP 842069

DOG FRIENDLINESS Under control on Ridgeway and on lead at Butler's Cross, Ellesborough and Great Kimble

PARKING Limited spaces at Butler's Cross

PUBLIC TOILETS None en route

In an age when politicians and world leaders live with the constant threat of terrorist attacks, it is perhaps a little surprising that you can take a country walk through the grounds of Chequers – the Prime Minister's official country seat near Princes Risborough. The Ridgeway cuts across its picturesque parkland, almost like a symbol of our democratic heritage, passing within sight of Chequers and offering superb views of the house and its glorious Chiltern setting.

Weekend Retreat or Veritable Fortress?

But don't be fooled. When the Prime Minister chooses Chequers to host a summit or entertain the Russian President, you can be sure that the security forces will have it sealed like a drum. Surveillance is usually discreet and understated – there might not be armed guards and security barriers as far as the eye can see, but you know you are being watched.

Take a walk in the surrounding countryside and chances are you'll strike up a conversation with people who claim to have seen police combing the woods in search of terrorists or cranks. Others say they have seen two identical convoys of ministerial cars and Special Branch 4x4 vehicles leaving Chequers one winter's day – one presumably carrying the Prime Minister and his staff, the other a possible decoy. Fact or fiction, it all adds to the romance and mystery of Chequers and provides plenty of fodder for writers of political thrillers.

Gifted to the Nation

Built in 1565, the house was given to the nation in 1921 by Viscount Lee of Fareham. He wrote: '...the better the health of our rulers the more sanely they will rule, and the inducement to spend two days a week in the high and pure air of the Chiltern hills and woods will, it is hoped, benefit the nation as well as its chosen leaders'. Lady Mary Grey, sister of the ill-fated Lady Jane, was initially confined here in disgrace by Elizabeth I after marrying Thomas Keys without her consent. Civil War battles were fought in this part of the country and the house contains one of the finest collections of relics from that period, though sadly they are not seen by the public.

Not all Prime Ministers have been impressed by Chequers. Bonar Law disliked the country, but Clement Attlee loved it and even bought a house in the area. Ramsay McDonald described it as 'this house of comforting and regenerating rest', but it was Churchill who summed it up best: 'What distinguished guests it has sheltered, what momentous meetings it has witnessed, what fateful decisions have been taken under this roof'.

WALK 13 DIRECTIONS

❶ From Butler's Cross follow Chalkshire Road, keeping the Russell Arms on the right. Walk along to a row of cottages and take the path opposite signposted 'Aylesbury Ring'. Cross four stiles, continue ahead and pass a path on the right. Continue to a drive on a bend and keep ahead, passing Springs Cottage. Ahead of you now are two stiles. Veer left to a further stile, and then swing left and head up the field slope to Ellesborough church. Cross a stile into the churchyard and keep to the right of the church. Over a stile, cross the road to a bus stop and veer right for several paces to go through a kissing gate.

WALK 13

❷ Follow the path diagonally up the slope to a kissing gate, sweeping round to the right of Beacon Hill. Make for a gate and continue through woodland, up a flight of steps to the edge of the trees. Cross a field at the top, heading for the next wood, and take the track between trees. Cross a track leading to Chequers, make for a kissing gate and initially follow the field boundary. After 100 paces, leave the wood on the left and stride out across the field to a waymark post and a kissing gate. To visit the Bernard Arms at Great Kimble, go through the gate and follow the Ridgeway down to the village. To continue the walk, bear left across the field to a kissing gate, now on the Ridgeway Path. Keep woodland on the right and Chequers in view across the field. Follow the path to a Ridgeway fingerpost waymark, cross the field and the drive to the house, crossing it via three gates, and continue to a kissing gate.

❸ Cross the road and follow the Ridgeway through woodland. On reaching a four-way junction, turn left and follow the path along the side of the hill. After 0.5 mile (800m), a number of paths converge. Turn left at the road, then right where it joins Missenden Road. Keep to the right edge and pass a lodge house. Follow the path north as the road diverges to the north-west. Continue through woodland to a gate. Bear left, leaving the National Trust land by a second gate. Follow the path and drive to the road by Coombe Hill Farm.

❹ Turn right, cross to a pavement and, after 100 paces, turn left to a barrier and join a long path half right up a large field. Bear right at a track, following it to the road opposite Ellesborough church. Enter the churchyard, keep to the right of the church and make for an iron gate. Pass some cottages on the left, go downhill to the pavement and return to Butler's Cross.

Coombe Hill Viewpoint

Follow woodland paths to a lofty monument for views in all directions.

See map and information panel for Walk 13

DISTANCE 6 miles (9.7km)   MINIMUM TIME 2hrs 45min

ASCENT/GRADIENT 165ft (50m) ▲▲▲   LEVEL OF DIFFICULTY ✦✦✦

START/FINISH Grid reference: SX 144519

WALK 14 DIRECTIONS
(Walk 13 option)

At the four-way junction where Walk 13 turned left, just after Point ❸, go straight ahead. This leads to a slightly longer alternative route back to Butler's Cross. Go straight ahead steeply up through the wood. Bear left at the next waymarked Ridgeway junction, Point Ⓐ, swinging right after several paces at the next sign. Keep to the left of a disused pit in the woodland and follow the Ridgeway Path waymarks through the trees. Cross a bridleway and keep right at a Ridgeway and footpath waymark. Continue through the trees and then alongside wooden fencing to a stile. Over this, bear immediately left and make for the next stile and kissing gate, out to the road, Point Ⓑ, still on the Ridgeway

Turn right and walk along to a cottage. Bear left and follow the Ridgeway through the trees. Turn left at the next path junction, and then swing right after 30 paces, avoiding the path running straight ahead, down the hill. Follow the path to the monument on top of Coombe Hill, Point Ⓒ, with magnificent views along this stretch over a sizeable area of Buckinghamshire. Chequers and the houses of Ellesborough are clearly seen from this viewpoint. Gliders often swoop silently into view in the skies above.

Coombe Hill represents the highest open space in the Chilterns, so it's hardly surprising that this lofty viewpoint, 843ft (257m) above sea level, was chosen to erect a memorial to the men of Buckinghamshire who died during the Boer War (1899–1902). The monument, seen clearly from the grounds of Chequers, was erected by public subscription in 1904. The ill-fated memorial was struck by lightning in 1938 and later rebuilt. In 1972 the bronze tablet attached to the memorial was stolen. A stone one replaces it.

Keep the monument behind you and, now no longer on the Ridgeway path, descend steeply to a gate on to the road at the foot of the hill. Cross over and follow the clearly waymarked path across the immaculate fairways of Ellesborough Golf Club. Walk ahead to a stile, skirt a field to the next stile on the left and over it follow the path across the field alongside a fence, then a hedge to the road, via a gate and a stile. Turn left and return to the start of the walk.

Overleaf: South Africa Monument on the top of Coombe Hill (Walk 14)

End of the Line at Chesham

Discover the delights of the little-known Chess Valley before returning to Chesham by tube.

DISTANCE	5 miles (8km)
MINIMUM TIME	2hrs 15min
ASCENT/GRADIENT	165ft (50m) ▲▲▲
LEVEL OF DIFFICULTY	✦✦✦
PATHS	Roads, field and woodland paths and tracks, 5 stiles
LANDSCAPE	Unspoiled farmland and woodland scenery of Chess Valley
SUGGESTED MAP	OS Explorer 181 Chiltern Hills North; 172 Chiltern Hills East
START/FINISH	Grid reference: SP 960016
DOG FRIENDLINESS	On lead in Chesham, Latimer and where there may be livestock, under control elsewhere
PARKING	Chesham tube
PUBLIC TOILETS	Chesham tube and Chalfont and Latimer tube

WALK 15 DIRECTIONS

If you're not familiar with the county of Buckinghamshire, it's something of a surprise to arrive at a small country town and find signs for the London Underground – the instantly recognisable circle with a line running through it. At Chesham's charming little station you can board a tube train and travel 25 miles (40.2km) to Aldgate in the City of London via places like Finchley Road, Northwood Hills, Wembley Park and Pinner – the heart of Metroland.

Chesham lies at the end of a branch of the Metropolitan Line,

which opened in 1889. Together with nearby Amersham, it's one of London Underground's furthest outposts. Work began on extending what was then known as the St John's Wood Line beyond central London during the latter years of the 19th century. By the mid-1880s the railway had become known as the Metropolitan, running 17.5 miles (28km) from Baker Street. The plan was to continue the line all the way to Aylesbury, but financial problems restricted its extension at that time to Chesham.

Most of the land for the new sections of railway was acquired from the Duke of Bedford and Lord Chesham, but the land for the final half mile (800m) of the Chesham branch was presented to the railway by local residents to enable a station to be built in the centre of the town instead of on the outskirts, as was originally planned. In May 1889 the people of Chesham were invited to inspect the branch and afterwards

WHAT TO LOOK OUT FOR

Latimer House, once the home of Lord Chesham, is now a conference centre. A short distance from Latimer Station lies the entrance to Beel House, the former home of the film star Dirk Bogarde (1921–99).

> **WHERE TO EAT AND DRINK**
> There are no pubs on the rural stretches of the walk, but Chesham offers plenty of choice – including the Last Post and the Cock Tavern.

entertained to a banquet. Seven weeks later, the line from Rickmansworth to Chesham was opened. For the next three years, until the main line from Chalfont and Latimer Station to Amersham and Aylesbury was opened in 1892, Chesham was the Metropolitan's most northerly terminus.

Turn left out of the station to join the Chess Valley Walk. The delightful old signal box can be seen from the path. Bear right at the waymark and walk down to Trinity Baptist Church. Cross the main road and follow the way through Meades Water Gardens to reach the road by a roundabout. Make for Moor Road on the far side and pass beneath the railway. When the road sweeps right, go straight on along a tarmac path alongside the River Chess. Swing right at the next footbridge and rejoin the road.

Pass a swimming pool and go straight over at the next junction, now back on the Chess Valley Walk, following the trail between the river and a recreation ground. Over a footbridge the path continues between branches of the river, crosses the river again by a weir and continues parallel to Latimer Road. Joining the road, continue past Milk Hall Barns and pass a footpath on the left and when it swings right at a bridge, veer off to the left to a stile, signposted 'Blackwell Hall'. Cross four stiles to reach the road. Swing left, passing Blackwell

Farm, and continue ahead on a track as the lane sweeps left. On reaching farm outbuildings, go straight ahead.

There are two tracks running parallel across the fields. Keep to the left track, go through a kissing gate and continue over farmland, passing through two kissing gates to reach a gate leading into the wood. Follow the path uphill, ignore a path on the right and continue through to the woodland edge. Skirt the field, keeping the trees on your right and head for a kissing gate. Walk towards a white gate for several paces, looking for a hedge and fence gap in the left boundary, out to the road.

Turn right, pass the entrance to Parkfield Latimer and follow the road down to the Old Rectory and the entrance to Latimer House, now the offices of De Vere Venues. Continue down the road past the church to the next entrance to the house and just beyond it join a tarmac drive running down into the valley via a kissing gate. Down by the weir the view to the north is dominated by the façade of Latimer House. When the drive forks, go through the kissing gate ahead and across the pasture to the road via a kissing gate.

Cross over to a kissing gate and follow the wide path half right up the field slope towards woodland. Bear right to pass through a kissing gate and about 75yds (69m) beyond it, veer left and climb between the trees. Cross a wide track and head for a house. Keep to the right of it and join a drive leading to a road. Follow Chenies Avenue, cross Elizabeth Avenue and head down to a junction. Bear left and walk along to the Chalfont and Latimer Station to catch the tube back to Chesham.

Jordens and its Waters of Peace

Visit a Quaker settlement and museum recalling the life of a famous poet.

DISTANCE 6.75 miles (10.9km) **MINIMUM TIME** 2hrs 45min

ASCENT/GRADIENT 98ft (30m) ▲▲▲ **LEVEL OF DIFFICULTY** ✦✦✦

PATHS Paths across farmland and some road walking, 6 stiles

LANDSCAPE Undulating farmland and woodland on edge of Chilterns

SUGGESTED MAP OS Explorer 172 Chiltern Hills East

START/FINISH Grid reference: SU 991937

DOG FRIENDLINESS On lead where signs request it and at Jordans

PARKING Car park off main street, almost opposite church

PUBLIC TOILETS In main street, near Milton's Cottage

A simple stone in a quiet burial ground in the Chilterns marks the grave of outspoken Quaker William Penn (1644–1718). There is nothing here that indicates what this man achieved in his lifetime – the founding of Pennsylvania in 1682.

Penn's Last Resting Place

Penn had a difficult life. Imprisoned several times for speaking out against religious principles, he always remained loyal to his beliefs. It was Penn who secured the release, in 1686, of almost 2,000 people imprisoned on religious grounds. He and his two wives, Hannah and Gulielma, together with ten of their 16 children, are interred in the burial ground beside the historic Meeting House. The house was built by Quakers in 1688 as soon as the Declaration of Indulgence, issued by James II, ended the persecution of Nonconformists. Step inside and, looking at the plain wooden benches and the walls decorated with portraits, it is as if time has stood still.

Jordens Farm

During the 17th century Old Jordens Farm, next door to the Meeting House, was a meeting place of the early pioneering Quakers, as well as the scene of religious persecution. The farm, whose history can be traced back to 1618, was inherited by William Russell, son of Thomas Russell, the sitting tenant. He eventually bought the freehold – the deed, complete with the thumb-prints of the principals and witnesses, used to hang at Old Jordans. Over 300 years ago William Penn worshipped here with fellow Quakers, but meetings were frequently broken up by order of the local court. Undeterred, these people continued to spread their message, often travelling to the far-flung corners of the country.

Old Jordans remained in Quaker hands until the early years of the 18th century. By 1910 the Society of Friends discovered that the farm, now virtually derelict, was up for sale. They acquired it the following year, members carrying out extensive improvements and adding a wing in 1920. In recent years a new building has replaced the old refectory.

CHALFONT ST GILES

Mayflower Timbers

On the south side of the garden lies the Mayflower Barn, originally the main barn of Old Jordens farm. The barn, built the same year the *Mayflower* was broken up, is said to contain timber from the ship. The dining room door at Old Jordens is also believed to come from the vessel which carried the Pilgrim Fathers to America.

Old Jordens closed as a Quaker guest house and conference centre. It used to attract visitors from all over the world and was called a 'well where men come to draw waters of peace'.

WALK 16 DIRECTIONS

❶ From the car park turn right and walk through the village. After 0.75 mile (1.2km), bear right into Back Lane, swinging left after a few paces. Through a kissing gate, keep left at the fork, avoid a stile in the boundary and continue to a wide gap in the hedge, just before the field corner. Cross into the adjoining field and continue to maintain the same direction, following the path for about 60yds (55m) to a hedge gap. Keep ahead in the next field, with the hedge on your left, and make for the next stile. Go through the hedge gap and cut across corner of next field, through another hedge gap

51

and half right to follow the clear path across the paddock via three gates, then between trees until you reach a stile and waymark.

② Turn left and skirt the field to a gate and stile amid trees. Continue ahead through trees to the next stile beyond which is a drive. Follow it alongside New Barn Farm to the road. Turn left and left again at the junction. Bear right just beyond a left bend and follow the waymarked track to Willow Court Stables. Go through a kissing gate and follow the fenced path alongside paddocks.

WHILE YOU'RE THERE

John Milton (1608–74), one of England's greatest poets, settled in Chalfont St Giles in 1665, fleeing the plague in London to finish *Paradise Lost* (1665). Today his home and garden are open to the public. The village was Walmington-on-Sea in the film version of *Dad's Army* (1971).

③ On reaching a path crossroads, turn right and pass through a kissing gate, under power cables. Make for a kissing gate and cross the recreation ground to the red dog waste bin. Continue ahead, cross the drive to Manor Farm and follow the wide tree-lined path. Head for a path junction and go straight ahead between houses. Cross Copse Lane and follow Seer Green Lane into Jordens village. Keep ahead to the junction and turn right towards Seer Green. Pass the former Jordens Quaker Guest House the Mayflower Barn

WHERE TO EAT AND DRINK

The Merlin's Cave pub in Chalfont St Giles offers the likes of liver and bacon, chilli con carne, bangers and mash, sandwich platters and oven-baked jacket potatoes.

and follow the road, and through kissing gates into the graveyard down to the Meeting House.

④ Turn left into Welders Lane and pass the entrance to a youth hostel. Continue along the lane to a track on the left, signposted 'Grove Farm'. Walk along to a kissing gate on the left, just before a private property sign, and head diagonally across a paddock, passing beneath power cables. Skirt the stables via three kissing gates and two stiles, turn right and follow the fenced path to a galvanised kissing gate. Keep along the wire fenced path and woodland edge, pass a public footpath on the right and continue to a junction by the corner of a wire fence.

⑤ Swing right, pass through the trees and bear left to a kissing gate by the road. Cross over and follow an enclosed path. Eventually you'll come down to a track by a bungalow called Brymavic. Cross over, through a gate, and continue on the path as it skirts a bowling green, playing fields and a recreation ground. Look for a path in the corner and keep to the right of a school. Go down to the road, turn right and return to the car park in Chalfont St Giles.

WHAT TO LOOK OUT FOR

The estate office at Jordens recalls the life and work of Fred Hancock, secretary of the village for 25 years. A plaque describes his achievements, and how he devoted himself to the maintenance and welfare of the village.

Disraeli's Des Res at Hughenden Manor

Visit the home of a famous British statesman on this scenic Chiltern walk.

DISTANCE *7 miles (11.3km)* **MINIMUM TIME** *2hrs 45min*

ASCENT/GRADIENT *280ft (85m)* ▲▲▲ **LEVEL OF DIFFICULTY** ✦✦✦

PATHS *Field, woodland and parkland paths, some roads, 3 stiles*

LANDSCAPE *Heart of Chilterns, north of High Wycombe*

SUGGESTED MAP *OS Explorer 172 Chiltern Hills East*

START/FINISH *Grid reference: SU 827950*

DOG FRIENDLINESS *On lead around West Wycombe and Downley, signs at various points request dogs be on lead or under control*

PARKING *Car park by church and mausoleum at West Wycombe*

PUBLIC TOILETS *Hughenden Manor, West Wycombe House*

Looking at Hughenden Manor's delightful setting on the slope of a hill and surrounded by woods and unspoiled parkland, it's not difficult to see why Benjamin Disraeli, Queen Victoria's favourite Prime Minister, chose it as his country home in 1848.

Born in 1804, the baptised son of a Spanish Jew, Disraeli was clever and ambitious. Fiercely political, his main objectives in life were to further the cause of the workers, popularise the monarchy and foster the might, unity and glory of the British Empire. His greatest political rival was the Liberal leader William Gladstone who disliked Disraeli's imperialism and his grand notions of empire.

Queen's Favourite

It was Disraeli who turned Queen Victoria against Gladstone, forging a close association with the Monarch at a time when she most needed the trust and support of others. After her beloved Albert died in 1861, Victoria withdrew from public life to mourn his loss. As the years passed, she became an increasingly distant and reclusive figure – isolated from her family and her subjects. Benjamin Disraeli coaxed her back, winning her trust and giving her the confidence she needed to continue as Queen. Towards the end of his life, he had become one of her closest confidants.

By the time he and his wife moved to Hughenden, Disraeli was an established novelist as well as a significant figure in British politics. As leader of the Conservative Party in the House of Commons, it was clear he was destined for higher office. Disraeli became Chancellor of the Exchequer in Lord Derby's three successive ministries and Prime Minister in the 1860s and 70s. Widowed in 1872, he was created Earl of Beaconsfield four years later, remaining at Hughenden until he died in 1881.

When Disraeli purchased Hughenden Manor, it was a white-painted, three-storeyed Georgian building of simple, unfussy design. The house was given a Gothic flavour by the architect E B Lamb in 1862, and the west wing was added by Disraeli's nephew, Coningsby.

53

WEST WYCOMBE

Now in the care of the National Trust, Hughenden contains most of Disraeli's books, pictures and furniture. There are manuscripts and letters from Queen Victoria who spent some time in Disraeli's study after his funeral. The display case in the Disraeli Room has a copy of Prince Albert's speeches and addresses, given by Queen Victoria in gratitude for his moving speech in the House of Commons following the Prince Consort's death.

WALK 17 DIRECTIONS

1 From the car park enter churchyard via a gate and pass to the immediate right of the church.

Continue to the mausoleum and line up with the A40 down below. Take the grassy path down the hillside, avoid the path on the right, make your way down to a fork, keep right to a flight of steps and descend to the road, emerging by the Hell-Fire Caves. Bear left and pass Church Lane on the right. Take the next path on the right via a kissing gate and keep to the right-hand boundary of the field. Look for a stile and maintain the same direction down to a stile by the road.

2 Cross over, make for a gate, pass under the railway and over a stile. At the field, go straight ahead keeping to the right of the fence. Follow the path to a hedge gap beyond a willow copse, cross a track and continue up the slope. Make for a stile by a gate and some barns. Through a fence gap, join a lane, swing right at the waymark and follow the ride through woodland. Eventually you reach a kissing gate beyond which the path crosses a field.

3 Go through a kissing gate to a track and turn right to cut through the wood. Veer left at

the fork and head for the road. Emerge at cricket pitch and bear left into Downley. Turn left for the pub or right to continue the walk. Pass some houses and when the track bends sharply left, go straight ahead to cross the common, following the path through clearings and into trees. On descending and reaching a National Trust sign, turn sharp left (not the bridleway signed 'Hughenden Valley') and follow the path through the woods. Avoid the path on the left and follow the white arrows. Pass a gate and continue ahead, up the moderately steep slope to a junction.

4 Keep right and follow the path to a track. Swing left to visit Hughenden Manor or right to continue the walk. Follow the path through woodland, then between fields, and make for tree cover. Entering the wood bear immediately left, up the slope through the trees, following the white arrows. Passing between the scout hut and a house turn right at the road. Pass the Bricklayers Arms and go straight over at the junction.

5 Keep ahead through the trees to a housing estate. Go forward for several paces at the road, bearing right at the first footpath sign, immediately past the school entrances. Follow the path as it bends left and runs down to a junction. Swing left for several steps, then veer right by some houses, heading down through trees to a galvanised gate. Take the sunken path to the right, follow it down to a fork and continue ahead. Head for a lane and follow it towards West Wycombe. Cross Bradenham Road and walk ahead into the village. Turn right into West Wycombe Hill Road and head up to the car park.

Turville on TV

*Climb into glorious woods and enjoy views you
may find familiar.*

DISTANCE *3 miles (4.8km)* **MINIMUM TIME** *1hr 30min*

ASCENT/GRADIENT *150ft (45m)* ▲▲▲ **LEVEL OF DIFFICULTY** +++

PATHS *Field and woodland paths, some road walking, 4 stiles*

LANDSCAPE *Rolling Chiltern countryside, farmland and woodland*

SUGGESTED MAP *OS Explorer 171 Chiltern Hills West*

START/FINISH *Grid reference: SU 767911*

DOG FRIENDLINESS *On lead around Turville and Skirmett and across farmland*

PARKING *Small parking area in centre of Turville*

PUBLIC TOILETS *None en route*

A visit to the delightful Chiltern village of Turville leaves you with the impression that you may have been here before – not in reality perhaps, but in the private world of fantasy and imagination. It's more than likely you have been to Turville without ever leaving your armchair.

Turville is one of Britain's most frequently used film and television locations. Its picturesque cottages and secluded setting at the bottom of a remote valley make it an obvious choice for movie makers and production companies. Over the years the village has featured regularly both on the large and small screen. Two notable productions in recent years have brought Turville to the attention of a new generation of television audiences. The BBC comedy *The Vicar of Dibley*, starring Dawn French in the title role, is filmed in the village and the tiny cottage by the entrance to the church doubles as the vicar's home. Back in 1998, the village was extensively used in the award-winning ITV drama *Goodnight Mister Tom* with the late John Thaw. This delightful wartime story was an immediate hit and Turville's classic village 'Englishness' was the programme's cornerstone.

Goodnight Mister Tom may have been set during the Second World War, but one of Britain's most famous propaganda movies, filmed at Turville, was actually shot during it. *Went the Day Well*, based on a short story by Grahame Greene, dates back to 1942 and illustrates how a small English village is captured by German fifth columnists. Several locals and ex-residents of Turville recall how they moved props on a handcart and pushed rolls of barbed wire on cartwheels, which were used in the film as blockades. The Old School House, by the green, was the local police station in the story.

Overlooking the village is Cobstone Mill, an 18th-century smock mill, which has also played a key part in various productions. The windmill was used in a 1976 episode of *The New Avengers* television series in which Purdey and Gambit, played by Joanna Lumley and Gareth Hunt, drive through the village in a yellow MGB, chasing a helicopter that lands by the windmill. Cobstone Mill was also used in the children's film classic *Chitty Chitty Bang Bang* (1968), starring Dick Van Dyke as Caractacus Potts, who transforms an old racing car into a wondrous flying toy. The family lived in the windmill.

WALK 18 DIRECTIONS

❶ Take the lane just to the left of the church entrance, with Sleepy Cottage on the corner. Pass Square Close Cottages and the village school before continuing on the Chiltern Way through a tunnel of trees. Climb gently to a gate and keep ahead along the field-edge to a second waymark in the boundary. Branch half left at this point, heading diagonally down the field to a stile.

❷ Cross the road to a further stile and follow the track through the trees, passing a gas installation on the right. Pass a bench on the left before breaking cover from the trees. Avoid a path branching off to the right and continue up the field slope to the next belt of trees. Turville and its windmill are clearly seen over to the left. Enter the woodland and keep left at the junction. Follow the clear wide path as it contours round the slopes, with the ground, dotted with beech trees, rippling away to the left. Descend the hillside, keeping to the woodland edge. Follow the fence and bear left at the next corner, heading to a stile by Poynatts Farm.

❸ Walk along the drive to the road, bear right and enter Skirmett. On the right is Cobs

Cottage and next door to it is the aptly-named Ramblers. Pass The Frog Inn and follow the road south to the next junction. An assortment of houses, a telephone box and a postbox line the route. Turn left, pass a stile on the right and walk along to the next left footpath. Go through a gate, follow the field-edge to a bungalow and gate, go through to a drive and make for the road.

❹ Bear right, heading out of the village to the junction with Watery Lane. 'Except for access' signs can be seen here now. Look for the gate and footpath immediately to the right of it. Cross the field to a half-concealed gate in the corner and make for the boundary hedge ahead in the next field. Through the gate, head diagonally right to a hedge by some houses. Through a gate turn right and follow the lane past a junction to Fingest and visit the church of St Batholemew. Out of same gate bear right at '30mph' sign on to the footpath via a gate. Flint wall gives way to hedge, then field.

❺ Through a gate cross the road to follow the Chiltern Way between trees, offering teasing glimpses of the Chilterns themselves. Cross a stile and head diagonally down the field towards Turville. Make for a track and follow it to the village green.

On Location in Hambleden

Opt for a long loop and head for another movie village.

See map and information panel for Walk 18

DISTANCE *9 miles (14.4km)* **MINIMUM TIME** *3hrs 30min*

ASCENT/GRADIENT *215ft (95m)* ▲▲▲ **LEVEL OF DIFFICULTY** +++

WALK 19 DIRECTIONS
(Walk 18 option)

Near the junction at the southern end of Skirmett, close to Stud Farm and between Points **3** and **4**, look for a gate on the right and follow the Chiltern Way, the Hamble Brook away on your right, crossing two stiles then going through three kissing gates and a gate to reach a house, Point **A**.

Cross a lane and keep to the left of the house and follow the path through the trees. Keep alongside a hedge, heading towards houses. Cross the field and continue on a track. Go straight on at the road, passing Colstrope Farm on the left. Look for a kissing gate on the right-hand bend. Continue ahead to a kissing gate and keep the field-edge on your right. Head for a kissing gate and continue, with the field-edge now on your left. Make for Pheasant's Hill through two kissing gates. Cross a drive to a further kissing gate and continue beside a paddock. Pass through two kissing gates, either side of a conifer belt, and cross the next field, a fence on your right, go through a kissing gate and veer left to another. Swing right on the road into Hambleden.

Like nearby Turville, this has become a favourite with film and television producers.

Stop off at the Stag and Huntsman Inn, and then retrace your steps, keeping the church on the left and the manor on the right. At Point **B** pass pairs of cottages and bear right where there is a footpath sign on the left signed 'Huttons Farm'. Follow the lane up the hill through the trees, and keep ahead between fields. Pass a kissing gate and then a stile on the left and continue towards outbuildings at Hutton's Farm. At the crest and past a barrier, bear sharp left just before them and go through a gate. Follow the track into woodland. Keep left at a waymarked fork leaving the metalled track, cross a track and continue ahead on a grassy path. Cross a stile and keep right at the road.

At Point **C** walk along to Rockwell End, swing left here and eventually pass a turning on the right for Marlow. Bear left just beyond St Katharine's, a retreat, following the tarmac lane to a house with a balcony. The lane dwindles to a path here and descends gradually between trees and bushes. Pass a path running off sharp right and then another before descending between hedges to the road. Keep left. Walk a few paces along the road down to the path on the right, skirt the field and rejoin Walk 18 at Point **4**.

The Meandering Thames at Marlow

Enjoy a pleasant mix of town and country on this attractive riverside walk.

DISTANCE 4 miles (6.4km)	**MINIMUM TIME** 1hr 30min
ASCENT/GRADIENT Negligible ▲▲▲	**LEVEL OF DIFFICULTY** ✦✦✦

PATHS Pavements, paved paths, lane, byway, field and meadow path, tow path, 1 stile

LANDSCAPE Thames Valley townscape and meadows

SUGGESTED MAP OS Explorer 172 Chiltern Hills East

START / FINISH Grid reference: SU 849865

DOG FRIENDLINESS On lead in Marlow and under control on Thames Path

PARKING Car parks in Pound Lane and Oxford Road, off West Street

PUBLIC TOILETS Behind Waitrose at river end of High Street

WALK 20 DIRECTIONS

A stroll through the streets of Marlow reveals many buildings of architectural and historic interest. From the tourist information centre turn right and make for the junction at the top of the High Street. Bear left into West Street, by the former Crown, now the Steamer Trading Company.

This popular hostelry dates back to 1807 and was originally built as the town's Market House, replacing a previous wooden building. Up on the first floor is an impressive Assembly Room. The original hotel, a renowned coaching inn, stood immediately to the right of the present building and is now shops and offices. The obelisk outside commemorates the Hatfield to Bath turnpike road.

Continue along West Street and pass the Premier Indian Restaurant (No 31) on the left, the home of T S Eliot between 1917 and 1920. Further on is Ye Olde Tuck Shoppe on the right and just beyond it are Shelley House and Shelley Lodge.

These houses, formerly one, in West Street were once the home of the poet Percy Bysshe Shelley, who lived here in 1817. He wrote much of *The Revolt of Islam* (1818) while out boating on the river. At this time his wife Mary, who had married Shelley when she was still a teenager, would be at home working on her classic story *Frankenstein* (1818). From here the couple moved to Italy.

Walk back along the road, almost to the Thai Square, and branch left at the sign for the Town Council

WHERE TO EAT AND DRINK

The Two Brewers pub, which was a popular haunt of Jerome K Jerome, who supposedly wrote part of *Three Men in a Boat* (1889) here, is a fine watering hole at the end of the walk. The emphasis is on modern European cuisine, and there is a choice of real ales.

Offices and the Thames. Follow the tarmac path and turn right at the next road junction. Head for Lower Pound Lane and a byway sign and pass hard tennis courts on the right and a cricket club on the left. Pick your way through the trees, cross a bridge and follow the tarmac track as it dwindles to a path.

Cross a stile, pass a sign for Quarry Farms and continue between fields and meadows. Make for Low Grounds Farm and keep left at the lane. Head for the Thames, with Quarry Hill and Winter Hill rising to meet the distant skyline. The buildings of Temple can also be seen ahead as you follow the lane towards the tow path. On reaching the river, swing left and follow the Thames Path towards Marlow.

Further downstream the buildings of Bisham Abbey edge into view on the opposite bank. Pass a welcome riverside seat and up ahead you will see Marlow's striking parish church. Pass the council offices and head towards All Saints and the town's famous suspension bridge which spans the River Thames, here forming the county boundary between Buckinghamshire and Berkshire.

The bridge, which was completed in 1832, was designed by William Tierney Clark who had designed the 1820s bridge at Hammersmith, in London, since replaced and the one across the Danube in Budapest. The Marlow and Budapest suspension bridges are now the only surviving examples of his work.

Back in 1965, long before most of today's television soaps were even thought of, the BBC broadcast a drama about daily life in a riverside hotel. The opening shots of *The Flying Swan*, which starred British film actress Margaret Lockwood and her daughter Julia, were filmed across the suspension bridge at the Compleat Angler, one of the south's most famous and exclusive hotels. Omar Sharif, Clint Eastwood and Naomi Campbell are among many celebrities that have stayed at the hotel over the years.

Rebuilt in 1835, All Saints Church occupies a delightful riverside setting at the bottom end of the High Street. There has been a church on this site since Saxon times and inside are many fascinating monuments, including one to Sir Miles Hobart, a parliamentary maverick who, in 1628, locked the door of the House of Commons until various taxation resolutions were passed.

Follow the High Street, with Marlow's war memorial and the George and Dragon seen over on the right. To visit the Two Brewers pub, take the alleyway on the right, just beyond the church. Head along the High Street, cross Station Road and look for Cromwell House on the right, once the home of Edwin Clark, a noted Victorian engineer. Continue along the street, back to the tourist information centre.

WHAT TO LOOK OUT FOR

Bisham Abbey, on the opposite bank of the Thames, presents a striking picture on the walk. Queen Victoria is said to have called here while out driving in her carriage, but found no one at home. The Tudor house, built by Sir Philip Hoby using fragments of the original abbey, is now the setting for the Sports Council's National Recreation Centre.

Burnham's Beautiful Beeches

Enjoy the spacious clearings and sunny glades of a National Nature Reserve, a welcome green lung in a bustling world.

DISTANCE *4.5 miles (7.2km)*   **MINIMUM TIME** *1hr 45min*

ASCENT/GRADIENT *150ft (46m)* ▲▲▲   **LEVEL OF DIFFICULTY** +++

PATHS *Woodland paths and drives, field paths, tracks and stretches of road, 3 stiles*

LANDSCAPE *Dense woodland and some open farmland between Slough and Beaconsfield*

SUGGESTED MAP *OS Explorer 172 Chiltern Hills East*

START/FINISH *Grid reference: SU 957850*

DOG FRIENDLINESS *Under effective control within Burnham Beeches and across farmland where there may be livestock*

PARKING *Car park at Burnham Beeches*

PUBLIC TOILETS *Burnham Beeches*

Before the Corporation of the City of London bought Burnham Beeches in 1880 for public use and enjoyment, it was described as an area of 'woodland and waste'. Up until that time it had been owned by the Grenville family of Dropmore and on the estate is East Burnham Cottage, where the dramatist Richard Sheridan (1751–1816) and his bride spent their honeymoon after they eloped in 1773. Here, he wrote to a friend: '…were I in a descriptive vein, I would draw you some of the prettiest scenes imaginable'.

Later, in the 19th century, historian George Grote lived here, entertaining such luminaries as Chopin, Mendelssohn, John Stuart Mill and singer Jenny Lind. It is fascinating to picture these characters strolling among the beeches and admiring their beauty.

Nature Reserve

Extending to 600 acres (243ha) and now a National Nature Reserve, Burnham Beeches contains the world's largest collection of ancient beech, with an average age of more than 300 years. The steward of the Hundred of Burnham, one of the original Chiltern Hundreds (Saxon administrative divisions), had an almost impossible job on his hands preventing highway robbery in and around these thick woodlands. The locals were very protective towards the beeches, treating them almost as if they were their own. When the corporation acquired Burnham Beeches, some people protested against the new bylaws in the strongest terms, attacking the keeper and throwing him into a pond.

Burnham Beeches was part of a huge forest that once stretched across the Chilterns in prehistoric times. Much of that woodland has disappeared over the years but the beeches at Burnham continue to remind us of that once thickly wooded landscape. The beech is one of Britain's most prolific trees and the county of Buckinghamshire is closely associated with what

BURNHAM BEECHES

was once nicknamed 'the Chiltern weed'. Native to southern England, the beech has shallow, expanding roots allowing it to thrive on thin soil where many other trees will not grow. Its thick foliage permits only a hint of sunlight to reach the ground beneath it, discouraging the growth of other plants. As a result, a classic beech wood has a floor thickly strewn with its own deep brown, perfectly sculpted leaves. Few of us, when out walking, can resist the temptation to kick our way through them on a glorious autumn day.

Burnham Beeches is perfect for walking. While many people stray little further than the end of the car park, it's very rewarding to plunge deep into the woodland, pausing to admire the wildlife and learn about the process of pollarding along the way. If time allows, you, too, may like to explore the area in greater depth.

WALK 21 DIRECTIONS

❶ Follow the drive away from Farnham Common, keeping the car parking area on the left. Pass a refreshment kiosk and veer right at the fork just beyond it. Soon reach a gate where you enter the National Nature Reserve's car-free zone. Follow Halse Drive as it curves left and down between trees. At the bottom of the hill swing left into Victoria Drive.

2 Follow the broad stony drive between the beeches, avoiding turnings either side of the route, and eventually reach a major junction with a wide path on the left and right. On the right is a large beech tree with 'Andy 6.9.97' carved on the trunk. If you manage to miss the path, you will soon reach the road. Bear right and go up the slope, keep left at the fork and cross several clearings to reach the road at the junction with Green Lane and Park Lane.

3 Cross the road to a stile and waymark and go straight ahead, keeping the boundary on your left. Make for a stile and descend into the field dip, quickly climbing again to pass alongside the grounds of Dorney Wood. Walk ahead to the field corner, cross a stile and turn right at the road. Head for a waymarked footpath on the left and cross the field, the hedge on your left, to a gap in the trees and hedgerow. Through the hedge, turn right and skirt the fields, making for a belt of trees and banks of undergrowth. The path cuts between two oak trees in the next field before reaching a gap in the hedgerow.

4 Turn left out to the road. Pass Common Lane and Horseshoe Hill and turn right at the next

bridleway. Follow the track through the wood to the next road at Littleworth Common. Go through a kissing gate to the right of the Blackwood Arms and follow the Beeches Way. Beyond a gate continue ahead between the wood and a wire fence and through a kissing gate before following a fenced path. Go through a kissing gate and take the path between the trees of Dorney Wood.

5 On reaching a kissing gate, cross over to the road and continue ahead on the Beeches Way. Make for the next major intersection and keep right along Halse Drive. Pass Victoria Drive and retrace your steps back to the car park.

Stoke Poges and a Garden Graveyard

Savour the peace and beauty of a cherished ornamental landscape before crossing Gray's Field to a striking monument.

DISTANCE *4 miles (6.4km)*   MINIMUM TIME *1hr 45min*

ASCENT/GRADIENT *Negligible* ▲▲▲   LEVEL OF DIFFICULTY +++

PATHS *Semi-residential paths and drives, field tracks and paths, some road walking and stretches over golf courses, 11 stiles*

LANDSCAPE *Partly residential, interspersed with golf courses and stretches of open countryside*

SUGGESTED MAP *OS Explorer 172 Chiltern Hills East*

START/FINISH *Grid reference: SU 977825*

DOG FRIENDLINESS *On lead on golf courses, in Memorial Gardens and churchyard and in residential areas*

PARKING *Opposite Memorial Gardens*

PUBLIC TOILETS *Memorial Gardens, closed evenings and weekends*

The dawn of the 21st century promised significant changes at Stoke Poges Memorial Gardens. Following a successful application to the Heritage Lottery Fund, money was made available to restore the gardens, preserving the rich mosaic of trees and shrubs.

A Peaceful Corner

The gardens were founded by Sir Noel Mobbs in 1930 on land that formed part of Stoke Park. Sir Noel's aim was to provide a corner of peace and beauty in an increasingly hectic world, and by the late 1930s they had been designed, landscaped and completed to everyone's satisfaction. The arrival of the motor car brought noise and pollution to the streets of Stoke Poges, but the gardens escaped the intrusive bustle of the 20th century. Today, they remain a haven of tranquillity .

The gardens were designed by Sir Edward White, one of Britain's leading landscape architects. Dedicated in 1935 as non-denominational memorial grounds, they were acquired by the local authority in 1971 and are registered as Grade II on the English Heritage Register of Parks and Gardens of special historic interest in England.

Among Flowers and Trees

The Memorial Gardens are regarded as unique in this country – one of the few surviving gems of the pre-war period that have stood the test of time. Even more heartening is that they are still in use today. Those who have loved the gardens in life often choose them as their final resting place. They buy a plot here so their ashes can be interred in beautiful surroundings, where flowers, trees and shrubs reflect the changing seasons and the constant, uninterrupted cycle of life. In short, this is a garden graveyard.

The grounds cover 20 acres (8ha) with 2,000 private gardens, including rock and water gardens, rose gardens, parterre gardens, heath gardens and individual specimen trees and shrubs. There are also formal gardens enclosed by yew hedges and informal gardens surrounded by glorious flowering shrubs. Running through the Memorial Gardens is the main avenue leading down to the colonnade, characterised by columns, water channels, magnolia trees and multi-coloured flower beds.

With over half a century behind them, the gardens have reached the stage where decay and disease are beginning to take their toll. Refurbishment work will restore the character and beauty of the Memorial Gardens for future generations.

WALK 22 DIRECTIONS

❶ From the car park, turn right and walk along the road. Before the pavement ends, cross over and look for a waymark and a kissing gate by an oak tree on the right. Go through the gate and follow the path as, initially, it

runs parallel with the road. Pass the entrances to various private houses and go through two more kissing gates before the path joins a residential drive – Duffield Park. Bear right when you get to the road junction and then take the first footpath on the left, by the sign for Snitterfield House.

STOKE POGES

WHAT TO LOOK OUT FOR

Stoke Poges church is usually open and inside you'll find evidence of Saxon, Norman, early Gothic and Tudor influences. At the western end of the church is what is known as the 'Bicycle Window'. The window depicts a figure sitting astride what appears to be some sort of ancient hobby-horse, which he pushes with one foot while playing a trumpet. It was designed as a Second World War memorial.

2 Follow the wide tarmac drive and, avoiding the stile on the left and the turning on the right, continue for several paces to a half-hidden right-hand stile just before the next sign for the house. Cross the paddock to a stile. Over it, make for the boundary, cross a stile and footbridge and then keep along the right edge of the field. Look for a stile by an oak tree in the corner and cross the next field via another stile to the road via two more stiles. Turn left, passing the hospital entrance. Just beyond it, on the right, is a private drive sign and an electricity transformer. Bear right here to a stile by gates and follow the track.

3 Cross the next stile after about 50yds (46m) and continue ahead to Bell Farm. Pass the outbuildings and keep ahead on a grassy track to a stile and gate. Cross a stile and turn left and follow a bridleway (Galleons Lane) to

a plank bridge and stile on the left. The walk now crosses a golf course. Cut across the fairways to a wide path and follow it to the club car park. Take the drive, veering right to a stile by a row of houses and follow the track to the road. Bear right and walk along to the Plough Inn.

4 Swing left into Plough Lane and when it bends right, go straight on along the public bridleway. Cross the next road to a kissing gate and continue on a waymarked path. Keep ahead, bearing left at pond, crossing the old driveway to Sefton Park via two kissing gates and then a golf course before reaching a kissing gate leading out to the road. Turn left and walk along to Rogers Lane on the right. Make for the kissing gate on the corner and follow the outline of the path ahead to a second gate.

5 Through the gate, branch half right and follow the path towards the Clock House and through four more kissing gates before reaching the road. Cross over to a kissing gate and follow the straight path across Gray's Field towards the monument. Keep to the right of the monument and look for the kissing gate leading into the churchyard. Walk through it to the car park.

WHERE TO EAT AND DRINK

The Plough at Wexham Street is a useful watering hole. Expect traditional home cooking, a Sunday roast and local real ales. There is a beer garden where you may like to relax on a summer's day.

WHILE YOU'RE THERE

Take time to look at the monument to Thomas Gray, poet and scholar. Gray's *Elegy Written in a Country Churchyard* (1751) has been described as our most famous poem and it was here at Stoke Poges that he composed the final lines. The monument was erected in 1799 by John Penn, grandson of William Penn (see Walk 16).

Dorney Court and England's First Pineapple

*Visit one of Buckinghamshire's oldest houses
and take a stroll by the Thames.*

DISTANCE 5 miles (8km)	MINIMUM TIME 1hrs 45min
ASCENT/GRADIENT Negligible ▲▲▲	LEVEL OF DIFFICULTY +++
PATHS Roads, firm paths and Thames tow path, 1 stile	
LANDSCAPE Lowland Thames valley	
SUGGESTED MAP OS Explorer 160 Windsor, Weybridge & Bracknell	
START/FINISH Grid reference: SU 938776	
DOG FRIENDLINESS On lead in Dorney and under control by Thames	
PARKING Large car park at Dorney Common	
PUBLIC TOILETS None en route	

Located in Buckinghamshire's most southerly village, close to the Thames, Dorney Court prides itself on being a genuine medieval village manor house. Motorways and modern housing estates grow ever closer, but the Grade I listed house with its jumble of timber-framed gables has survived intact and unchanged for almost 600 years, looking much the same today as when it was first built.

Fruit and Honey

The village of Dorney stands on a gentle rise in the Thames flood plain and is cut off from the river by spacious meadows where evidence of prehistoric life can be found. The name Dorney means 'island of bumblebees' and the local Dorney Court honey is renowned for its delicate, light flavours.

But it is not just honey for which the house is justly famous. The large carved stone pineapple standing in the corner of the Great Hall commemorates the first pineapple to be grown in England. The story suggests that the top of a pineapple, imported from Barbados, was sliced off at a dinner in the City of London and given to the Earl of Castlemaine's gardener to plant at Dorney Court. The pineapple thrived and was subsequently presented to Charles II in 1661. Nobody can be sure if it really happened but it makes a good story.

Medieval Manor House

Back in the mid-1920s, *Country Life* described Dorney Court as 'one of the finest Tudor manor houses in England'. Few would dispute that label and what endears the house to so many people is its long tradition of continuous family occupation – more than 450 years.

The first owner was recorded after the Norman Conquest and after changing hands several times in the 15th century, the house was sold in 1504 for 500 marks. By the middle of the 16th century the manor, together with 600 acres (243ha), was owned by Sir William Garrard, Lord Mayor of London. It is through this family that the town of Gerrards Cross got its name. Sir William Garrard's daughter Martha married Sir James Palmer of

DORNEY

Kent and Dorney Court has remained in the Palmer family to this day. One family portraits depicts Jane Palmer, born in 1564 and a forebear of Diana, Princess of Wales. The layout of the house has changed little, although work has been undertaken to restore furniture and paintings.

WALK 23 DIRECTIONS

❶ From the car park turn left to follow the road across Dorney Common, towards Dorney village. Pass Wakehams, a timber-framed house with a well situated at the front. Away to the right is a fine view of Windsor Castle and its famous Round Tower. Keep left at the T-junction, cross a cattle grid and join the pavement. Walk

through Dorney, keeping the
Palmer Arms on your right. Bear
left into Court Lane, follow the
path parallel to the road and pass
the entrance to Dorney Court.
You soon reach the Church of
St James the Less.

❷ Continue on the path now on
the left side of the lane and when
the road bends right, go straight
ahead at the sign for Eton College
Rowing Centre. Keep to the right-
hand side of the drive and follow
the parallel path as it sweeps away
to the right by a plaque and a car
park. The path curves past the
end of the rowing lake and over a
footbridge. Make for some trees
and reach the Thames Path by a
Sustrans waymark.

❸ Turn left here and follow the
national trail, keeping Bray Marina
on the opposite bank. Further
downstream the imposing cream
façade of Bray film studios edges
into view, its sweeping riverside
lawns and weeping willows
enhancing the elegant scene.
Continue on the leafy Thames Path

and soon catch sight of Oakley
Court across the water on the
Berkshire bank.

❹ Beyond the hotel can be
seen the cabin cruisers and gin
palaces of Windsor Marina and
next to it lines of caravans and
mobile homes overlooking the
river. Through the trees on the
Buckinghamshire bank is the
outline of Eton College's new
boathouse and its superb rowing
lake. To gain a closer view, briefly
follow a path beside the river
boathouse and slipway, through
a gate walk towards the lake and
then retrace your steps to the
Thames Path. On the opposite
bank of the river is Windsor
Race Course Yacht Basin and
ahead now is the Chapel of
St Mary Magdalen. Follow the
path alongside the chapel to a
kissing gate and about 50yds
(46m) beyond it reach a lane.
With the Old Place opposite and
an avenue of chestnut trees on
the right, turn left and return to
the car park.

Thames Path to Eton Wick

Follow the river to Boveney Lock within sight of Windsor on this longer loop.

See map and information panel for Walk 23

DISTANCE 7 miles (11.3km) **MINIMUM TIME** 2hrs 45mi

ASCENT/GRADIENT Negligible ▲▲▲ **LEVEL OF DIFFICULTY** ✦✦✦

WALK 24 DIRECTIONS
(Walk 23 option)

Boveney Lock is said to stand by the site of a former fishery known as Gills Bucks, after the fish traps or bucks owned by Tom Gill. There was a dispute over an unpaid toll here in 1375. There were unsuccessful attempts to create a modern lock here, and it was not until the 1830s that Boveney Lock was opened. The present lock was constructed alongside the earlier one.

At Point **Ⓐ** keep the Chapel of St Mary Magdalen on the left and continue downstream along the Thames Path, heading for Boveney Lock. Windsor Racecourse can be seen over on the Berkshire bank.

The Thames, historically the most important river in Britain, has been used as a highway since early times. A stroll along its banks is surely the best way to appreciate its character, beauty and ever-changing scenery. The Thames Path, officially opened by the Countryside Commission in 1996, is the only long distance national trail in the country to follow a river for its entire length.

More than 95 per cent of the trail currently follows the intended route by the Thames, which rises in a Gloucestershire meadow near Cirencester. Despite problems over prohibited access in several places, the Thames Path has come a long way since the 1920s when the concept of providing public access to the countryside led to the eventual designation of the route in 1989.

Continue on the tow path, cross Boveney Ditch on a footbridge and bear immediately left at a path junction. The modern Windsor spur road can be seen over on the right, with the magnificent chapel of Eton College rising triumphantly above it. After 50 paces turn left over the footbridge by the distinctive Sustrans milepost and veer immediately right. Skirt round the field, keeping the ditch hard by you on the right, and pass a row of houses on the far bank. A waymark edges into view further on as the path now follows the Cress Brook, Boveney Ditch having turned north.

At Point **Ⓑ**, on reaching the field corner, swing left at the waymark and continue along the perimeter. Look for a footpath sign on the right and turn right to follow it between fields to a stile. Cross the common to the road and bear left, following it back to the car park at Dorney Common.

Royal Windsor

*Follow the scenic Thames from Windsor to Datchet
and return by train.*

DISTANCE 2.5 miles (4km) **MINIMUM TIME** 1hr 15min

ASCENT/GRADIENT Negligible ▲▲▲ **LEVEL OF DIFFICULTY** ✚✚✚

PATHS Pavements, drive, tow path, path across meadows and playing fields

LANDSCAPE Lowland meadows and town outskirts in Thames Valley

SUGGESTED MAP OS Explorer 160 Windsor, Weybridge & Bracknell

START / FINISH Grid reference: SU 968772

DOG FRIENDLINESS On lead in Windsor and Datchet, under control elsewhere

PARKING Car park at Riverside Station, Windsor

PUBLIC TOILETS Riverside Station, Windsor

WALK 25 DIRECTIONS

From Windsor and Eton's Riverside Station, turn right to the river bank where you will find River House, formerly the Donkey House pub overlooking the Thames. Pass through a set of wrought iron gates and follow Romney Walk, restored in 1993 by Windsor Heritage. The land for this footpath was presented by the Southern Railway Company in 1934. To the right are the car park and buildings of Windsor and Eton Riverside Station, where the Royal Waiting Room dates back to 1849. There are good views from here up to Windsor Castle, as well as glimpses of Eton College and its chapel through the trees.

Windsor Castle was founded as a fortress by William the Conqueror and has been substantially altered and extended over the centuries. The most recent work followed the much publicised fire in 1992. During his reign George IV spent nearly £1 million on improving the castle. The dominant feature is its Round Tower, built by Henry II and visible for miles around. Parts of the castle are open to the public, though the state apartments are closed when the Queen is in residence.

With its legendary reputation, Eton College still represents one of this country's great institutes of learning – Gladstone described it as the 'Queen of Public Schools'. On its famous playing fields, according to Wellington, the Battle of Waterloo was won.

In May 1990 the college celebrated its 550th anniversary.

WHILE YOU'RE THERE

Frogmore House, set in the private Home Park, is renowned for its splendid landscaped garden and 18th-century lake. Queen Victoria wrote of it: 'All is peace and quiet and you only hear the hum of bees, the singing of the birds'. She built a mausoleum for herself and her husband, Prince Albert, in the garden. Frogmore is open to the public on a limited number of days during the year.

It was founded in 1440 by Henry VI. Eton is modelled on Winchester College, and is the second oldest public school in the country. Originally it accommodated 70 poor scholars who were educated free of charge. The boys of Eton College still wear black tailcoats in mourning for George III, their favourite monarch.

Eton College chapel is similar in many ways to the chapel of Kings College, Cambridge, also founded by Henry VI. It was built between 1449 and 1482 and the chapel you see here today was originally to have been the choir for a much larger, more majestic place of worship. The splendid vaulted ceiling and the impressive 15th-century wall paintings are two of the college chapel's most distinguished features. Raised 13ft (4m) above ground, the college chapel is safe from flooding should the Thames burst its banks.

At the end of Romney Walk continue ahead on a drive, pass a cottage dated 1898 and an octagonal building dated 1912, which houses the waterworks for Windsor Castle. On reaching a boatyard, make for the water's edge and go through a kissing gate to walk along the grass tow path beside the river. Eton College Boathouse is soon seen on the opposite bank. Pass under the 19th-century Black Potts railway bridge and skirt the playing fields on the right. As you approach the next bridge, veer right to the far end of the white railings.

Turn left and follow the pavement over Victoria Bridge. Over to the right is the Home Park. Bear right on the far side and follow the Thames Path through the trees, with delightful views of

the Thames and the Home Park beyond. On reaching the road, via a footbridge, turn right along the B470 and then bear left into Queens Road which leads into the centre of Datchet.

This pleasant riverside village has strong literary associations. The main road to Windsor, at the southern end of the High Street, was the Datchet Lane in William Shakespeare's comedy *The Merry Wives of Windsor* (1602). Falstaff was transported along this road on his way to face a ducking in the Thames. The village is also mentioned in Jerome K Jerome's *Three Men in a Boat* (1889).

Just before the turn of the 20th century, and again soon after the Second World War, Datchet suffered serious flooding when the swollen Thames caused a pond in the centre of the village to overflow. Walk along to the green, turn right into High Street and head to the railway station for your return train.

Sunningdale and a Constitutional Crisis

Skirt the grounds of Edward VIII's favourite home on this attractive walk to exclusive Wentworth and Coworth Park.

DISTANCE 4 miles (6.4km)	**MINIMUM TIME** 1hrs 45min
ASCENT/GRADIENT Negligible ▲▲▲	**LEVEL OF DIFFICULTY** +++
PATHS Enclosed woodland paths, estate drive, paths and tracks, path across golf course and polo ground, no stiles	
LANDSCAPE Semi-residential area	
SUGGESTED MAP OS Explorer 160 Windsor, Weybridge & Bracknell	
START/FINISH Grid reference: SU 953676	
DOG FRIENDLINESS On lead across golf course and polo ground	
PARKING On-street parking in Sunningdale village	
PUBLIC TOILETS None en route	

In the closing weeks of 1936 newspaper headlines were dominated by one of the saddest and most dramatic chapters in the history of the monarchy – the abdication of Edward VIII, the uncrowned King who chose to give up the throne for the love of a woman, American divorcee Wallis Simpson.

Constitutional Crisis

He knew his decision would provoke the strongest disapproval – that what he wanted to do would be at odds with courtly tradition and principles. But Edward stuck to his guns. He was in love with Wallis Simpson, who was not allowed to become Queen because she had been divorced, and he had no intention of giving her up.

Fort Belvedere

During the crisis, played out against the backdrops of the House of Commons and the House of Windsor, Edward spent much of his time at Fort Belvedere, his beloved country residence near fashionable Sunningdale. Originally constructed by William, Duke of Cumberland, as a triangular belvedere tower in the 1730s, the building was later enlarged to become a miniature fortress for royal tea parties, the home of a royal collection of guns and for storing various family treasures. A battery of cannon was even installed, to be fired on royal birthdays by a resident bombardier. 'It was a child's idea of a fort', wrote Diana Cooper, a leading figure in royal circles and high society, 'the sentries, one thought, must be of tin'.

It was back in the 1920s, years before the crisis, that the Prince of Wales asked his father if he could use Fort Belvedere. Something of a playboy, Edward was a noted socialite who liked to entertain regularly and on a lavish scale. He was allowed to take up residence here, but in later years the house became much more than just a country retreat.

In the closing stages of the crisis, Edward asked his brothers to visit him at Fort Belvedere and witness his signature on the abdication document. It was signed at 12:45pm on Thursday 10 December, 1936 in one of the

King's private rooms. A few members of his secretarial staff were present and outside, on the Ascot road, a crowd gathered to see him leave the fort for the last time.

Happiest Days

Long after he had given up the throne and gone into exile, Fort Belvedere still occupied his thoughts. In his memoirs, Edward wrote fondly of the house that 'laid hold of me in so many ways'. When he finally drove away from Fort Belvedere, it seemed to him like a symbol of all he was giving up. 'The Fort had been more than a home', he wrote, 'it had been a way of life for me… it was there that I passed the happiest days of my life'.

WALK 26 DIRECTIONS

❶ From the Nags Head turn left and walk down the High Street, keeping the Anglican church on your right and the Baptist church on the left. Pass Church Road and continue along Bedford Lane.

Cross a brook and turn right immediately past some bungalows to follow a path cutting between hedgerows and fields. At the A30 bear left and walk along to a sign on the right for Shrubs Hill Lane and Onslow Road.

② Follow the leafy path to a junction by a closeboard fence and turn right by the bridleway/footpath sign. Curve left, make for a roundabout and swing left, looking for the footpath next to a house called Highgate. Follow it through the woodland and when you join a wider path on a bend, keep left. Skirt the golf course, going left of a substation, cutting between trees and bracken, and when you emerge from the woodland, follow the path across the fairways, keeping left at a junction by a bunker. Veer right at the first fork, into the trees, and follow the path, a fairway to your left. The path becoming tarmac swings left and across the fairway to a junction with a tarmac drive at a footpath signpost.

③ Turn left and pass through the Wentworth Estate, cutting between exclusive houses with secluded landscaped grounds and imposing entrances. On reaching the A30, turn left and follow the road west. Walk down to the Berkshire/Surrey border and bear sharp right, just before the Bluebells Restaurant, to join a right of way, initially gravelled, past South Lodge. Follow the shaded woodland path between beech trees and exposed roots. Beyond the wood you reach the buildings of Coworth Park.

④ Draw level with a stone bridge, turn left and follow the well-defined footpath alongside a post and rail fence across a broad expanse of parkland, part of which is used as a polo ground, crossing a track on the far side. Enter woodland, turn left at the road via a gate and pass several houses. When you reach the speed restriction sign, bear right to join a byway by Sunningdale Bowling Club. Keep to a tarmac drive and continue ahead. Turn left at the road, swinging left after 20 paces at the fork. Pass Coworth Road and return to the centre of Sunningdale village.

Windsor's Great Park

Royal footsteps on the Long Walk.

DISTANCE 5.5 miles (8.8km)	**MINIMUM TIME** 2hrs 30min
ASCENT/GRADIENT 160ft (49m) ▲▲▲	**LEVEL OF DIFFICULTY** +++
PATHS Park drives and rides, woodland paths and tracks	
LANDSCAPE Sprawling parkland of Windsor Great Park	
SUGGESTED MAP OS Explorer 160 Windsor, Weybridge & Bracknell	
START/FINISH Grid reference: SU 947727	
DOG FRIENDLINESS Dogs under strict control or on lead	
PARKING Car park by Cranbourne Gate	
PUBLIC TOILETS None en route	

Walkers in East Berkshire who enjoy peaceful parkland, leafy paths and a sense of space in a noisy and cluttered world don't have to look very far to find what they want. Right on their doorstep is the opportunity to walk for miles and yet remain within the confines of Windsor Great Park, once part of a royal hunting ground and now, in effect, an enormous nature reserve covering thousands of acres, where many different animals – deer among them – roam freely and undisturbed amid the ancient trees.

Windsor Great Park stretches south from Windsor Castle for about 5 miles (8km), almost as far as Chobham Common in Surrey. Comprising about 4,800 acres (1,944ha) of wooded parkland and magnificent landscaped gardens, the general design and landscaping is largely the work of George III's uncle, the Duke of Cumberland, who was given the rangership of Windsor Great Park in recognition of his victory over the Jacobites at the Battle of Culloden in 1746.

One of the park's most striking features is the oak-lined Long Walk, running in a straight line between Windsor and the mighty equestrian statue of George III on Snow Hill, erected in 1831 and known as the Copper Horse. Many members of the Royal Family have followed the Long Walk over the years, among the most recent royals to do so, in front of gathering crowds and television cameras, was Sophie, Countess of Wessex, who travelled by car through the Great Park in 1999, on her way to St George's Chapel where she married Prince Edward.

Copper Horse

The statue of the Copper Horse offers one of the most photographed views in Britain – that of Windsor Castle. During the late 1950s, the exiled Duke of Windsor described the royal residence and its surroundings thus: 'there is one place… which hardly changes at all, and that is Windsor Castle. Here is a palace essentially English in character. I take pleasure in the way it broods, with an air of comfortable benevolence, down over the homely town of Windsor, while to the south spreads the spacious Great Park, with the Long Walk stretching three miles through the soft, green English landscape and the meadows of the Home Park to the south, refreshed by the waters of the slowly winding Thames'.

But it is not just royals and ramblers who have loved Windsor Great Park over the years. Writers have been captivated and inspired by it, too. Alexander Pope often rode here and was moved to write about the scenery, Jonathan Swift reported that Queen Anne was 'hunting the stag till four this afternoon', while Swift described the Long Walk as 'the finest avenue I ever saw'.

WALK 27 DIRECTIONS

❶ From the car park, cross the A332 to Cranbourne Gate and enter the park. Follow the drive alongside trees planted over the years to commemorate Queen Victoria's Golden Jubilee in 1887 and Edward VII's coronation in 1902. Over to the left are distant views of Windsor Castle.

Turn right at the first crossroads, signposted 'Cumberland Lodge', and follow the drive to the next junction by two ponds where swans are often seen.

❷ Keep left here, signposted 'The Village'. Pass the Post Office and General Store, walk between a spacious green and a playing field and then turn right to join Queen

Anne's Ride heading towards an equestrian statue. Look back for another view of Windsor Castle, framed by the houses of The Village. Pass alongside Poets Lawn and follow the ride to a tarmac drive and the equestrian statue of the Queen erected for her Golden Jubilee. Turn left, keep left at the fork, then left again after a few paces at a crossroads.

3 Poets Lawn is now on your left. Continue ahead at the next intersection and then, beyond the woods, turn right to follow a broad, hedge-lined footpath. Ahead lies Royal Lodge and to the left of it is the famous Copper Horse statue. Take the next grassy ride on the left and head for a deer gate. Through this, keep ahead towards the statue and when you draw level with it, bear left. The figure of George III points the way. Follow the woodland path which merges with a clear sandy track running down to a drive. Pass through the automatic gate or the kissing gate and keep right at the immediate fork.

4 Walk along to Queen Anne's Ride, which crosses the drive just before a house. On the left is the millstone. Bear right here and follow the ride to Russel's Pond. Veer left away from the ride at this point and keep alongside the pond and fence. Walk ahead between fields and make for woodland. Drop down to the road at Ranger's Gate. Cross over at the lights and take the tarmac drive beyond the car park.

5 Veer half left about 100yds (91m) before some white gates and follow a sandy track alongside a field and up the slope and through the wood. Keep to the sandy track and, after 0.5 mile (800m), at the point where it bends left, go straight on along a path between trees. As it reaches a gate, turn left and keep alongside a fence. The path can be rather overgrown in places in summer. Follow the fence to a drive and on the right is the outline of Cranbourne Tower. Bear left and return to the car park.

Overleaf: Windsor Great Park and The Long Walk entrance to Windsor Castle

Danger Lurked at Dusk in Maidenhead Thicket

A pretty walk through extensive woodland,
once the haunt of highwaymen.

DISTANCE *3.5 miles (5.7km)*   MINIMUM TIME *1hr 30min*

ASCENT/GRADIENT *82ft (25m)* ▲▲▲   LEVEL OF DIFFICULTY +++

PATHS *Field and woodland paths, some road walking*

LANDSCAPE *Mixture of farmland and woodland to west of Maidenhead*

SUGGESTED MAP *OS Explorers 160 Windsor, Weybridge & Bracknell;*
172 Chiltern Hills East

START/FINISH *Grid reference: SU 838800 (on Explorer 172)*

DOG FRIENDLINESS *On lead across farmland and under control in woodland*

PARKING *By green in village of Littlewick Green*

PUBLIC TOILETS *None en route*

Maidenhead Thicket is one of those delightful places that you might frequently pass by in the car without even realising it's there. From the road, only a curtain of trees is visible, but step into Maidenhead Thicket and at once you are in a tranquil world of dense woodland and sunny glades. Lime trees, oaks and horse chestnuts bring colour and life to the well-used paths and tracks, and for a few short weeks every year the ground is covered with violets and hazy blue carpets of bluebells.

Haunt of Highwaymen

Maidenhead Thicket consists of 368 acres (149ha) of woodland and glades. These days it is National Trust land, but it is probably best known as a notorious haunt of highwaymen. The trees and bushes lining the Great West Road would have given these 18th-century muggers perfect cover as they lay in wait for passing stage coaches.

Nearby Maidenhead once boasted scores of inns which prospered on the vulnerability of coach passengers. Most opted to stay in the town overnight rather than risk driving through the dreaded thicket at dusk. It is also claimed that the highwaymen who lurked under the trees preferred the coaches entering the town from the west. Those approaching from the east had already been robbed by the highwaymen of Hounslow Heath.

Dangerous Times

Claude Duval (1643–70), one of the best-known highwaymen, preyed upon travellers in this area. According to a handbook on Berkshire, Buckinghamshire and Oxfordshire, published in 1860, 'in the reign of Elizabeth, the vicar of Hurley, who served the cure of Maidenhead, was allowed an extra salary to atone for the danger of passing the thicket'. Dick Turpin (1705–39) travelled this way too, waiting in the shadows to ambush any passing coaches. From here he galloped to his aunt's cottage at nearby Sonning where he stabled his horse, Black Bess, before going into hiding in Oxfordshire until the dust settled.

MAIDENHEAD THICKET

Black Mask

Jackson's *Oxford Journal* for 1 November, 1755 tells of a typical hold-up: 'Last Tuesday about 12:00 at noon, the Oxford machine (the stage coach from London), in which were three gentlemen, was stopped by a single highwayman, well mounted, with a black mask, in Maidenhead Thicket. Upon demanding their money, the passengers gave him about 12 guineas. He then demanded their watches, which two of the gentlemen delivered, but one of them desiring he would return the seal, on which was his coat of arms. The highwayman, observing that the watch was only pinchbeck, said it would be of little service to him and returned it. He then made off into the thicket'.

WALK 28 DIRECTIONS

❶ Head for the south-east corner of the green in the centre of Littlewick Green, continue into School Lane and follow it to the woodland edge. Emerging from the trees, bear left to join a made-up, tarmac track running across the fields, with a hedge on your left. There are good views to the south along here. Cross a road leading to a business park and continue over farmland to the next road. Turn left, pass an assortment of houses lining the route and walk almost to the A4, keeping right at the junction just before it.

❷ Cross over and enter Maidenhead Thicket, following the waymarked path between trees and clearings, soon merging with one from the left. On reaching a muddy bridleway, veer right and follow the main route along to the next junction, a footpath crossroads. This represents the site of Robin Hood's Arbour. Turn left here and follow the hard path to reach the lodge to Stubbings House on your left.

❸ Cross to the kissing gate to the right of it and then follow the path out across the fields through two kissing gates. The footpath, initially with a hedge on your left, graduates to a track before arriving at the buildings of Stubbings Farm. On reaching the road at Burchett's Green, turn left and pass some houses, one of which has a white weatherboarded dovecote tower. Follow the lane and veer half right just beyond the entrance to Old Oak Farm.

❹ Follow the path between hedgerows and trees and further on it runs alongside houses and bungalows. Along this stretch the path broadens to a track. The sound of traffic on the A4 gradually becomes audible.

At the junction go straight over into Jubilee Road and follow it towards the cricket ground at Littlewick Green. On reaching the edge of the green, bear right to join a waymarked footpath running alongside the ground and past the front of Littlewick Green cricket club. At the road turn left, passing the Cricketers Inn. Alternatively, follow the road round the eastern edge of the green to the start.

On to Hall Place

Cross picturesque grounds to reach woodland on the slopes of Ashley Hill.

See map and information panel for Walk 28

DISTANCE *7.5 miles (12.1km)*	**MINIMUM TIME** *3hrs*
ASCENT/GRADIENT *262ft (80m)* ▲▲▲	**LEVEL OF DIFFICULTY** ✦✦✦

WALK 29 DIRECTIONS
(Walk 28 option)

At Point **Ⓐ**, turn right at the road and keep the Crown on the left. Cross over into Hall Place Lane, keeping left at the entrance to Lane End House. Take the path to a gate and cross the field to trees. Reaching the lime avenue turn left and head towards Hall Place and swing right in front of the house.

Hall Place is Georgian and until the Second World War was owned by the Clayton East family. Sold to the Ministry of Agriculture, the house and part of the estate were acquired by Berkshire County Council in 1949 for the Berkshire Institute of Agriculture, later the Berkshire College of Agriculture.

Follow the drive to reach the vet's and veer half left just beyond it at the waymark. Once clear of the enclosures, pass between trees and bushes to a crossroads. Keep left at the fork just beyond it and follow the clear track towards woodland. Make for a galvanised gate and through the kissing gate to its right take the path to the far end of the wood, swinging left to follow the fence. On reaching a pair of gates and a waymark, turn left and cut back through the wood. Make for another kissing gate and then continue ahead between fields, towards the tree-clad slopes of Ashley Hill, crossing a track crossroads.

At Point **Ⓑ**, cross two tracks and go through a gate, crossing the field to a kissing gate. Follow the waymarked path through a belt of trees to the next kissing gate and at the top of steps continue along the field-edge. Pass a house and go through a kissing gate to the road. Turn right and follow the woodland edge. Go straight ahead at the bend, passing the turning to the Dewdrop Inn. Continue ahead at a 'private' sign and follow the path to a waymarked junction. Bear left, up through trees. Pass over a cross track and keep left at the fork. Ahead is the entrance to Clifton, an isolated house. Turn left here and follow the drive down through the woods. As it eventually sweeps to the right, go straight on to the road, Point **Ⓒ**.

Keep right and, when the road begins to curve to the right, look for a footpath branching left through the trees. Go through a kissing gate and skirt a fence and stream. Follow the path over a track by a gate and keep ahead towards houses. Cross a stile ahead on to the road and look for two paths opposite. Cross the road cut through the wood to Furze Cottage. At the road turn right and head for Old Oak Farm at Point **❹** on Walk 28.

Stanley Spencer's Cookham

A spectacular stretch of the Thames Path to Bourne End, returning by train.

DISTANCE 6 miles (9.7km)   MINIMUM TIME 3hrs

ASCENT/GRADIENT Negligible ▲▲▲   LEVEL OF DIFFICULTY +++

PATHS Pavements, riverside promenade, Thames Path

LANDSCAPE Riverside, fields and meadows

SUGGESTED MAP OS Explorer 172 Chiltern Hills East

START/FINISH Grid reference: SU 887807

DOG FRIENDLINESS On lead in Maidenhead, Cookham and Bourne End

PARKING Maidenhead Station

PUBLIC TOILETS Maidenhead Station

WALK 30 DIRECTIONS

From the car park walk down to the clock tower, erected to mark Queen Victoria's Diamond Jubilee in 1897. Cross the road at the lights and bear right into Queen Street, by the Bell pub. Veer right into York Road and pass the football club. Walk down to the mini-roundabout and turn left into Forlease Road. Head for the next junction and turn right into Moorbridge Road.

Walk along to the underpass and veer right on the far side, following Bridge Road towards Maidenhead Bridge. Pass some almshouses and a sign for the Thames before reaching the bridge. Cross the bridge almost to the opposite bank and look downstream to the right. Straddling the river is Brunel's famous railway bridge. Return to the Maidenhead side of the river and bear right into Ray Mead Road. Make for Boulter's Lock and continue to the point where the road and the Thames Path part company. Follow the tow path. The view to the Buckinghamshire bank is dominated by the beautiful hanging beech woods of the Cliveden Estate. Soon the sound of traffic fades as the walk turns its back on Maidenhead, following the Thames towards Cookham.

Eventually the path swings away from the river bank and cuts through woodland, eventually bearing left to continue alongside a drive, to reach a barrier. Cross over and veer slightly left, keeping to the right of a house. Head for a tarmac drive and turn left opposite Sol Mill. Walk along to the junction, bear right and follow the road into Cookham.

WHERE TO EAT AND DRINK

Maidenhead and Cookham offer a good choice of pubs and eating places. You might like to stop off at Jenner's Cafe near Boulter's Lock. Hot food is served all day, including full breakfast, and there are hot and cold drinks and ice cream. If you have to wait for the train back to Maidenhead, call into the Firefly pub next door to Bourne End Station.

The village will forever be associated with the artist Stanley Spencer who died in 1959. Spencer was a controversial eccentric figure and even now, more than 40 years after his death, his work is the subject of speculation and debate. He was born in Cookham High Street in 1891 and spent most of his life in the village. The former Methodist chapel on the corner of the High Street and the A4094 is now a gallery devoted to his work.

It was to this chapel that Mrs Spencer marched young Stanley and her eight other children every Sunday. Officially opened in 1962, the gallery exhibits many of Spencer's paintings, including *The Last Supper*, painted in 1920, and the view of Cookham from Englefield, completed in 1948. There is also an extensive collection of drawings, including much of his early work. *The Fairy on the Waterlily Leaf* and *Roy*, from 1909 and 1906 respectively, are here.

In addition to examples of Spencer's highly individual style, there is a permanent collection at Cookham of his letters, documents and notes, together with the pram in which Spencer wheeled his paints and brushes when painting landscapes. He was often seen pushing it around the village. Cookham played a key role in Spencer's work, forming the setting for many biblical and figure paintings, as well as landscapes.

Cookham Moor, the parish church and the High Street are all shown on canvas. The Sandham Memorial Chapel at Burghclere south of Newbury contains murals inspired by Spencer's experiences in the First World War.

Pass the Stanley Spencer Gallery and continue along the road, passing the Tarry Stone. Veer left at the entrance to the church, pass the memorial stone to Spencer, keep to the left of Holy Trinity and walk through the churchyard to rejoin the Thames Path via a gate. Swing left and pass Cookham Reach Sailing Club via two gates. Cross the meadow and keep close to the water's edge and go through kissing gate into the National Trust's Cockmarsh. Up ahead is Bourne End railway bridge.

Through kissing gate, pass beneath the bridge and turn immediately left, go up the steps and cross the footbridge to the Buckinghamshire bank. Once over the bridge and through a gate, turn right and pass a house called River Haven. Keep left at this point and follow the drive alongside a high brick wall to the road. Turn left and walk along to the station at Bourne End to catch the train back to Maidenhead.

Colourful Wargrave

Leave bustling Wargrave and head for
peaceful Bowsey Hill.

DISTANCE *6 miles (9.7km)* **MINIMUM TIME** *2hrs 15min*

ASCENT/GRADIENT *248ft (76m)* ▲▲▲ **LEVEL OF DIFFICULTY** ✦✦✦

PATHS *Stretches of road, field and woodland paths, 6 stiles*

LANDSCAPE *High ground on upper slopes of Thames Valley,*
dense woodland and peaceful glades

SUGGESTED MAP *OS Explorer 171 Chiltern Hills West*

START/FINISH *Grid reference: SU 786785*

DOG FRIENDLINESS *On lead near livestock and where requested by signs*

PARKING *Public car park in School Lane, just off A321*

PUBLIC TOILETS *At car park*

The riverside village of Wargrave is usually quiet during the week, but often busy with visitors and boating enthusiasts at the weekends, particularly in the summer. It is sometimes mistakenly believed that the village has a connection with military cemeteries. That couldn't be further from the truth – its name actually means 'grove by the weirs'.

The village is distinctly Edwardian in appearance but its origins date back many centuries. When Edith, the wife of Edward the Confessor, held the manor in the 11th century, it was known as Weregrave. The church among the trees dates from the First World War, replacing an earlier building that, except for the Norman tower, was destroyed by fire on Whit Sunday, 1914. It is believed that the fire was the work of a militant wing of the Suffragettes – angry because the vicar would not withdraw the word 'obey' from the marriage service. However, this claim was never proved. Madame Tussaud's daughter-in-law is buried in the churchyard.

Colourful Residents

Thomas Day, the 18th-century idealist, was a resident of Wargrave. He wrote Sandford and Merton (1783–9), the story of two boys – one rich, the other poor. Day was an eccentric character but a genial man, nonetheless. He supported the abolition of slavery and the protection of animals from cruelty. He believed, too, that animals responded to kindness and gentleness. However, this proved to be his undoing. One day in 1789, in an attempt to demonstrate his conviction, he mounted an unbroken horse and was subsequently thrown off and killed.

Wargrave seems to have produced more than its fair share of colourful characters over the centuries. One of them was Zachary Allnutt who lived for more than 100 years at Lavender Cottage on the Henley road. Allnutt was a well-known local lavender grower in the 19th century.

Another eccentric local figure was the 18th-century Irish peer, the Earl of Barrymore. He built a theatre close to his Wargrave home and engaged the services of a famous Covent Garden clown known as Delphini. The opening night in 1791 was a sensation, with the cream of theatrical society in attendance. The Earl died suddenly in 1793, and by that time he had frittered away over £250,000 on the theatre, as well as various other sporting pleasures. There is a final, rather sordid, footnote to this story. The Earl was buried at Wargrave church on a Sunday so as to prevent his creditors seizing his body and holding it until his debts had been settled!

WALK 31 DIRECTIONS

❶ Turn left and walk along School Lane, the B477. On the first bend, bear left into Dark Lane, head up the hill and turn right at the T-junction. Follow the road and turn left at the sign for Crazies Hill. Bear right by East Lodge, follow the lane to a bend and bear left through a gate to join a waymarked path. Keep alongside the fence, and then strike out across the fields towards trees. Through a gate turn right at the road, veering left through a kissing gate opposite a private house, Crouch End.

2 Now on a golf course, keep close to the left boundary of the field then descend steeply to a kissing gate and a bridleway beyond. Cross a stile almost opposite and climb the hillside. Over a stile at the crest keep ahead on the higher ground, following the path alongside the fence. Descend to a kissing gate at the road and turn immediately right. Head uphill and pass Worley's Farm.

WHILE YOU'RE THERE

As you approach Crazies Hill look across the fields towards nearby Cockpole Green. It is believed there was once a cockpit here where cock fighting took place.

3 Take the next waymarked path on the right, just before a row of trees, and over a stile. Walk between fences and hedges, going through a kissing gate near the crest, lining up with a large white house in the distance. Keep to the left of the house, Crazies, whose portico was salvaged from the old Henley Town Hall. Go through a kissing gate and follow an enclosed path to the road. Turn right, then left beside the village hall and, after a few paces, bear left by the old Old Clubhouse. Follow the path by a paddock to a kissing gate by the road. Bear right, past the entrance to Thistle House and a restricted byway into trees on the right.

4 Continue for several paces to a gate on the left. Join a woodland path and look out for white arrows on the tree trunks, eventually reaching a waymarked junction. Turn right here, avoid a

WHAT TO LOOK OUT FOR

The pretty hamlet of Crazies Hill lies on the upper slopes of the valley. There is a rather charming story behind its name. Apparently, buttercups were once commonplace in this area and 'crazies' is a rustic country name for buttercups. Look out for the entrance to Thistle House. In the 1960s this was the home of David Greig, a butcher who began a supermarket chain. His emblem was the thistle and the house was used as a training college for a while.

path on the right and keep going to the next waymarked junction, on the edge of the wood. Fields are visible here. Bear left and walk down to a flight of steps and a footbridge. Make for the woodland perimeter and turn right along the field edge.

5 Cross a bridleway via two stiles and continue ahead along the woodland edge. Look for a hedge gap on the right, cross into the adjoining field and maintain the same direction. Make for a kissing gate and a footbridge in the field corner and continue ahead to the remains of a wrought iron kissing gate. Follow the path across the next field, heading towards trees. Make for a kissing gate leading out to the road and turn right. Follow it down to the A321, turn left and walk along to School Lane.

WHERE TO EAT AND DRINK

There are several pubs in Wargrave – among them The Bull, The Greyhound and The White Hart. If you want to stop midway round the walk, try the Horns at Crazies Hill. This popular timber-framed pub has a range of filled baguettes and daily-changing menus.

Water and Wildlife at Dinton Pastures

This fascinating walk mostly stays within the boundaries of a popular country park, visiting six different lakes along the way.

DISTANCE *3 miles (4.8km)*	MINIMUM TIME *1hr 30min*
ASCENT/GRADIENT *Negligible* ▲▲▲	LEVEL OF DIFFICULTY +++

PATHS *Lakeside and riverside paths, some road walking*

LANDSCAPE *Extensive lakeland*

SUGGESTED MAP *OS Explorer 159 Reading, Wokingham & Pangbourne*

START/FINISH *Grid reference: SU 784718*

DOG FRIENDLINESS *Dogs under control and on lead where requested*

PARKING *Large car park at Dinton Pastures*

PUBLIC TOILETS *Dinton Pastures*

Dinton Pastures Country Park describes itself as a mosaic of rivers, meadows, lakes and woodland. The lakes were once gravel workings that were flooded to form the focal point of this attractive recreational area. Paths and self-guided trails enable visitors to explore this tranquil world of water and wildlife at will.

The Early Days

The park's river meadows were once farmed by Anglo-Saxons who called the area Whistley – 'wisc' meaning marshy meadow and 'lei', a wooded glade or clearing. The River Loddon was also used as part of the same process, farmed for its supply of eels, caught in willow traps for the monks of Abingdon Abbey. Traps were still in regular use as late as the 1930s.

By the beginning of the 17th century, much of the area formed part of Windsor Forest, where the monarch and his courtiers hunted for pleasure. It was the courtiers who built some of the region's grandest houses, including High Chimneys, which was handy for Windsor Castle, the royal powerhouse. High Chimneys' farmhouse, which later became the Tea Cosy café, dates back to 1904. During the mid-1920s it was occupied by a farmer who named the farm after his home village of Dinton, near Aylesbury.

Dinton Pastures forms part of the Loddon's flood plain and is a rich source of gravel, which has been extracted here for more than 100 years. There was an extensive extraction programme here during the late 1960s and right through the 1970s. Much of the material was used to construct the M4 and the A329(M), connecting Reading and Wokingham.

Recreational Area

Comprising about 230 acres (93ha) and opened in 1979, Dinton Pastures attracts many visitors who come here to walk, fish, picnic and indulge in birding – a welcome green space on Reading's doorstep. The largest of the lakes at Dinton Pastures is Black Swan. The Emm Brook once flowed where the lake is now situated. It was later diverted and the oaks which you can see on the island in the lake were once on the banks of the old stream.

DINTON PASTURES

All the lakes draw a variety of wetland birds such as swans, geese, coots and moorhens. The park's rarest birds are bitterns – less than 20 pairs breed in Britain annually. Several fly here in winter and in spring migrants such as nightingales also make the journey from Africa to nest at Dinton Pastures. The park offers all sorts of surprises – you may spot a weasel or a stoat, catch sight of a mink in the Loddon, or identify one of 18 species of dragonfly in the lakes and rivers.

WALK 32 DIRECTIONS

❶ With the Dragonfly café on the right and the exhibition centre and High Chimneys behind you, cross the car park to the site map. Follow the wide path and keep right at the fork by the 'wildlife trails' sign. Pass an enclosed play area on the left, keep the Emm Brook on the right and enjoy the tantalising glimpses of Black Swan Lake up ahead.

❷ Swing left on reaching the water and follow the path alongside the lake. When it veers right, turn left across a bridge to a sign for Tufty's Corner. Bear right here and keep left at the fork after a few paces. Follow the path beside White Swan Lake to a waymark post by a patch of grass and a flight of steps. Avoid the steps but take the left-hand path and follow it to the lake known as Tufty's Corner. On reaching a

DINTON PASTURES

junction by a bridge, turn right and keep the River Loddon on your left.

❸ Walk along to the next bridge. Don't cross it; instead continue on the riverside path. White Swan Lake lies over to the right, glimpsed at intervals between the trees. Further on, the path curves to the right, in line with the river, before reaching a sign 'private fishing – members only'. Join a track on the right here and bear left. Pass alongside Herons Water to a sign 'Sandford Lake Conservation Area' and Black Swan Lake. Turn left and keep Sandford Lake on the right. When the path curves right, go out to the road via a kissing gate.

❹ To visit the Berkshire Museum of Aviation, bear left and pass Sandford Mill. Take the road signposted 'No Through Road' on the left, pass several cottages and continue ahead when the road dwindles to a path. The museum is on the left. Retrace your steps to Sandford Mill and keep walking ahead to a footpath and kissing gate on the left. Through this, keep left at the first fork, then right at the second and head for the Teal Hide. Return to the road, cross over and return to the lakeside path.

❺ Continue with Sandford Lake on your right. On reaching a sign 'Sandford Lake – wildlife area – dogs under control' veer left over a bridge and turn left. Black Swan Sailing Club can be seen on the left. Continue on the broad path and look out across the lake to Goat Island, noted for its population of goats. On reaching the picnic area overlooking Black Swan Lake, turn left and retrace your steps back to the main car park.

WHAT TO LOOK OUT FOR

Sandford Mill, built in 1772, was in use until the mid-1950s and in 1994 it was converted into a private property. A mill was originally recorded on this site in the Domesday Book. With the trees surrounding it and its picturesque white weatherboarded façade, it creates a pretty picture in this corner of the park.

WHILE YOU'RE THERE

Visit the Tealhide at Lavell's Lake, overlooking the wader scrapes. See if you can spot wading birds from here – look out for the green sandpiper and redshank, ducks, swans, kingfishers and the occasional bittern. This site is for serious ornithologists. Not long ago this corner of the park was a meadow grazed by cattle or cut for hay, though the landscape changed dramatically at the time of gravel extraction. Take time to visit the Berkshire Museum of Aviation, just off the main route of the walk. The museum is dedicated to the contribution the county has made to flying. A Second World War hangar, newly extended and reclad, has been moved here from Woodley and there are various aircraft representing Berkshire's aviation history from the last 60 years or so.

Wokingham to the Country

*Discover a typical market town before heading
for open countryside.*

DISTANCE 6 miles (9.7km)	**MINIMUM TIME** 2hrs 30min
ASCENT/GRADIENT Negligible ▲▲▲	**LEVEL OF DIFFICULTY** +++

PATHS Streets, forest and field paths, tracks, I stile

LANDSCAPE Town streets and well-wooded countryside

SUGGESTED MAP OS Explorer 159 Reading, Wokingham & Pangbourne

START/FINISH Grid reference: SU 812685

DOG FRIENDLINESS Under control in woodland, on lead by paddocks

PARKING Public car parks in Rose Street and Denmark Street

PUBLIC TOILETS Rose Street and Denmark Street

A classic market town, Wokingham is full of hidden corners and picturesque old buildings. Before starting this walk, get hold of a good street map and an informative booklet on the town and head off in search of the real Wokingham.

Founded in the 13th century by the Norman-French Bishop Roger le Poore, the town was granted a charter by Queen Elizabeth in 1583. Until the 19th century Wokingham developed at a slow pace, but in recent years it has grown enormously, its rapid expansion influenced by its close proximity to London and the M4.

At the heart of Wokingham, in its Market Place, stands the impressive Town Hall dating back to 1860. It was designed in the Gothic revival style. Originally, the Town Hall was a police station, a courtroom and a gaol. If you stand outside and look closely, you can spot 'County Police Station' inscribed in stone near the top of the building.

Just a stone's throw from the Town Hall lies Rose Street, one of Wokingham's hidden treasures and the finest example in Berkshire of a medieval 'enclosed' street. Founded in the early 13th century, Rose Street is wide at one end and narrow at the other. At the far end stands All Saints Church, originally a small Saxon chapel that was enlarged in the 12th century. James 'Sooty' Seaward lived in Rose Street and was the inspiration for Tom the chimney sweep, the central character in Charles Kingsley's classic *The Water Babies* (1863).

At the far end of Broad Street and dating from the mid-16th century is the Tudor House, one of Wokingham's most historic and attractive buildings. Until the end of the First World War, the building housed a school. Next to the Tudor House is Wokingham Police Station, built in 1904 to the design of the county architect. The distinctive pagoda-style tower complements the building's chimneys. Running south-west from the Market Place is Denmark Street, which still evokes memories of old Wokingham. Many of the houses here were built in the 15th, 16th and 17th centuries. The Duke's Head pub at the bottom of the street was originally three cottages with a pond at the back used for tanning hides.

Reading ← A329

Wokingham

A329 Bracknell →

Station

Ship Inn

Town Hall

①

B3349

Dukes
Head

⑤ School

Tesco's

A321

astheath

**Chapel
Green**

**Holme
Green**

—N—

② Ludgrove
School

Lucas
Hospital

Golf
Course

**Gardeners
Green**

The Throat

③

A321

*Queen's
Mere*

④

Heathlands
Court

Site of
Who'd a
Thot it
PH ✝

Heathlands

B3430

*Heath
Lake*

Ⓐ

B3430

*King's
Mere*

Ravenswood
Village

Dormy House

Golf
Course

Crowthorne

Diligence

Ⓑ

*Heath
Pond*

0   ½ mile

0   500 m

Ⓒ

B3348 Station

↓ Sandhurst

B3348

Wellington
College

97

WALK 33 DIRECTIONS

1 With the Town Hall on your right, walk down Denmark Street. Pass the Wokingham Memorial Clinic and keep right at the Duke's Head. Walk to the roundabout, cross Kendrick Close and follow Finchampstead Road. Pass under the railway and take the footpath on the left at the next roundabout, just before Tesco. Head for a gate, veer right by some loose boxes and follow a fenced track. Make for a line of houses and continue to Lucas Hospital, a fine building of 1665.

2 Look for a stile here and head diagonally right across the paddock to a tarmac drive leading to Ludgrove School. Turn right, pass some white gateposts and bear left just beyond them at a pair of galvanised gates. Begin a lengthy stretch of track walking, keeping the railway line on your right. Eventually pass an old wartime Nissen hut and a cottage on the right. Continue for about 80yds (73m) and then turn right by some wooden posts.

3 Follow the straight track between plantations, ignoring tracks left and right. Avoid the path ahead at the left-hand bend and keep right at the next fork. Pass a gate, make for the road and turn left. Pass Kingsbridge Cottages and Grove Close before reaching the site of a former pub, now flats (St Sebastian's Court). Continue along the road to St Sebastian's Church, and turn left into Heathlands Road. Pass the entrance to Heathlands Court and swing left just beyond it to join a byway by a sign for Bramshill Forest.

4 Swing right at the next waymarked junction by a

galvanised gate and when the path bends right, go through a deer gate and carry on across market gardens and out through another deer gate. Continue between fences and fields and follow the path to the left of an entrance to Ludgrove School. Cut between laurel bushes and holly trees, go through a gate and cross a drive leading to the school and continue towards Wokingham. Keep ahead to a railway footbridge and veer right on the far side, following Gypsy Lane.

5 Pass Southfields School, cross Erica Drive and continue on Gypsy Lane to the next main junction. Cross Murdoch Road and follow Easthampstead Road towards the town centre. Bear right at the T-junction and walk along to the Ship Inn. Keep left here, following Wiltshire Road, and turn left into Rose Street. Follow it back to the Market Place.

Right: Tudor House, Wokingham

Wellington at Crowthorne

Skirt the playing fields of an historic public school on this longer walk.

See map and information panel for Walk 33

DISTANCE 8 miles (13.6km)   **MINIMUM TIME** 4hrs 15min

ASCENT/GRADIENT Negligible ▲▲▲   **LEVEL OF DIFFICULTY** +++

WALK 34 DIRECTIONS
(Walk 33 option)

On reaching Nine Mile Ride, the B3430, between Points ❸ and ❹ on Walk 33, turn right at Point ❹, cross the railway bridge and walk down to the roundabout. Cross Lower Wokingham Road and turn into Hollybush Ride. King's Mere can be seen on the right. Pass a house called Diligence on the left and continue ahead at an intersection of tracks.

This is part of Finchampstead Ridges, 60 acres (24ha) of lovely woodland, including a heather ridge and an extensive network of paths, cared for by the National Trust. The area has much to interest the naturalist and ornithologist, with spotted flycatchers and siskins among the species seen here. If time allows, you may like to take a stroll and explore the attractive scenery.

At Point ❸, with Heath Pond on the right, turn left and at the next track junction bear right to follow the byway, keeping right at the gates to a property called Heritage. Follow the track to a roundabout and take the second exit for Crowthorne. On the right are the playing fields of Wellington College.

One of Britain's most famous public schools, Wellington College dates back to the mid-19th century when it was founded as a memorial to the Duke of Wellington, following his victory at Waterloo in 1815. When it first opened, it was a school for the orphans of army officers. The railway station was originally known as Wellington College Station but changed its name after the First World War when Crowthorne began to expand.

Pass the railway station and a line of shops before turning left into Ravenswood Avenue, at Point ❸. Walk along to the East Berkshire Golf Club, established in 1904, and follow the drive as it runs across the fairways. Look for a footpath sign and continue with the course now on your right. Pass a house called Dormy House and take the next left footpath, following it along the woodland edge. Join a tarmac drive and pass alongside the buildings of Ravenswood Village, a community providing care for children with learning difficulties. Head for Nine Mile Ride, crossing over into Heathlands Road. Rejoin Walk 33 at Point ❹ and follow the route back to the centre of Wokingham.

Left: The Heathlands (Walk 33/34)

Finchampstead and Word of a Royal Bride

Enjoy a very pleasant country walk where kings and princes once hunted.

DISTANCE 3.5 miles (5.7km)	**MINIMUM TIME** 1hr 30min
ASCENT/GRADIENT Negligible ▲▲▲	**LEVEL OF DIFFICULTY** ✚✚✚
PATHS Mainly field paths and tracks, 7 stiles	
LANDSCAPE Classic farmland on northern side of Blackwater Valley	
SUGGESTED MAP OS Explorer 159 Reading, Wokingham & Pangbourne	
START/FINISH Grid reference: SU 793638	
DOG FRIENDLINESS On lead where there is livestock	
PARKING In vicinity of Finchampstead church and Queen's Oak	
PUBLIC TOILETS None en route	

WALK 35 DIRECTIONS

From the Queen's Oak turn right towards the church, following the footpath sign. Keep right as the lane forks and soon dwindles to a stony track, descending through a wooded tunnel. Pass the entrance to Manor Beacon, cross the next road via two kissing gates and follow the path between bracken and hedges. Make for a waymarked junction of paths and go straight on through a barrier, keeping several gates on the right.

Follow the clear path as it cuts between fields and through woodland. Keep alongside a hedgerow to a stile and out to a lane. Cross over to a kissing gate and skirt the field, keeping the fence on your immediate right.

WHERE TO EAT AND DRINK

The Queen's Oak is handy for a drink and something to eat. Snacks and other fare are available and there is a large enclosed beer garden at the side, pleasantly shaded by trees.

Head for a kissing gate ahead, and then another gate to pass between trees to the road and turn right. Bear left at the sign for Vann House and follow the track to Fleethill Farm. Keep to the left of the outbuildings, cross two stiles and continue alongside the woodland edge, initially along a track, then beyond a stile as a path, to a pair of stiles in the field corner. Bear left after a few paces and follow the path between trees, joining a drive on the edge of Finchampstead.

This stretch of the walk is along an ancient road. According to some sources, it was here, in November 1501, that Henry VII and his sons Arthur and Henry, rode to meet Catherine of Aragon following her arrival from Spain. The King and the two princes had been hunting near by when they learnt that Catherine had reached Henry's hunting lodge at Dogmersfield.

Years earlier, Henry VII had dreamed of a marriage alliance with Spain. The youngest daughter of Ferdinand and Isabella of Spain,

FINCHAMPSTEAD

WHILE YOU'RE THERE

Step into Finchampstead church, built on an ancient earthwork with a steep scarp on three sides. Over the chancel arch are fragments of 12th- and 15th-century wall paintings.

Catherine was born in December 1485. She was just nine months older than Prince Arthur. When Catherine was nearly three years old, a treaty was signed which permitted them to marry when they were both of a suitable age. A member of the powerful Spanish royal family, Catherine was addressed as 'the Princess of Wales' from a very early age. She spent many years preparing for the day she would finally leave Spain and set sail for England. Eventually that day dawned, and in September 1501, Catherine began her journey. She would never return to her native Spain. On her arrival at Plymouth, she heard Mass and gave thanks for her safe passage. Meanwhile, a messenger began the lengthy journey to the King's residence at Easthampstead to inform his majesty that the long wait was over.

When word eventually reached Henry and his two sons, they made their way to Dogmersfield, arriving there on the evening of 4 November. But Catherine had

retired for the night and would see no one. Deeply suspicious, Henry insisted on seeing her and eventually his wish was granted. Lifting her veil, he was relieved to discover Catherine was a pretty girl, with red gold hair, blue eyes and a fair complexion.

Ten days later, on 14 November, 1501, Catherine and Arthur were married in St Paul's Cathedral. He was just 15 and she was nearly 16. Little did Catherine realise what lay ahead. Arthur died six months after the wedding and his father passed Catherine on to his younger son, Henry, who duly married his brother's widow in 1509. As the Church forbade such a union, a special dispensation was obtained from the Pope. By about 1527, Henry, now King, was desperate for an heir, but all his children by Catherine, with the exception of one, had died in infancy. Having met and fallen in love with Anne Boleyn, Henry VIII was anxious to dissolve his marriage as soon as possible. The Pope refused to bow to his wishes and it was this decision that eventually triggered the Reformation in England.

Take the first left turning on to a footpath, passing alongside a fence and beneath the boughs of holly trees. Turn left by the garage over a low stile and walk along to a drive on the right for Rectory Farm. Follow it to a kissing gate and path to the right of the main gate, bear right after about 60yds (55m) and cut between paddocks. Go through a gate, followed by a footbridge, turn left, then right. Swing left at the next junction by some steps and head for Finchampstead church. Cut through the churchyard via a kissing gate and return to the Queen's Oak.

WHAT TO LOOK OUT FOR

Close to the Queen's Oak is another royal connection. Encased by creeper is a plaque which reads: 'The oak tree near this stone was planted 21 June 1887 in commemoration of Queen Victoria's completion of the 50th year of her reign'. The stone was placed here in June 1897 to mark her Diamond Jubilee.

A Walk on the Wilde Side of Reading

Enjoy a heritage trail that explores the heart of Berkshire's county town, following parts of the Thames and the Kennet and Avon Canal.

DISTANCE *3 miles (4.8km)*   **MINIMUM TIME** *1hr 15min*

ASCENT/GRADIENT *Negligible* ▲▲▲   **LEVEL OF DIFFICULTY** ✚✚✚

PATHS *Pavements, river and canal tow path, no stiles*

LANDSCAPE *Urban*

SUGGESTED MAP *OS Explorer 159 Reading, Wokingham & Pangbourne. AA Street by Street Reading*

START/FINISH *Grid reference: SU 716735*

DOG FRIENDLINESS *On lead in town, under control on river bank*

PARKING *Reading Station, Chatham Street, Garrard Street, Hexagon*

PUBLIC TOILETS *Reading Station*

Reading's skyline has changed dramatically over the years – riverside office developments have taken the place of many of the older buildings and the vast, Oracle shopping complex is now the glittering jewel in the town centre's crown. However, some of old Reading's landmarks remain – and one of them is the town's gaol where Oscar Wilde languished for 18 months, between November 1895 and May 1897.

Importance of Being Oscar

It was the 8th Marquess of Queensberry, frustrated by thwarted attempts to break up the scandalous relationship between his son, Lord Alfred Douglas, and Wilde, who was responsible for the writer's downward spiral. He had publicly insulted Wilde, at his home, at his clubs and throughout London's theatreland where many of Wilde's plays were staged.

Caught in the crossfire between father and son, Wilde brought a prosecution for libel against Queensberry, though he lost the case. Queensberry and his cohorts now began plotting to destroy Wilde. They gave evidence against him, testifying to his dubious sexuality and improper practices. The 1885 Criminal Law Amendment Act made sexual relations even between consenting males illegal and Wilde was found guilty.

After two short spells in London prisons, Wilde was transferred to Reading Gaol. By now his physical condition had deteriorated and he was depressed and confused. Impressed by Wilde's reputation as a gifted writer, the governor made arrangements for him to work in the garden and the prison library. But life was still very tough in gaol.

If prison's dreary routine was hard for Wilde, things were no better on the outside. His books were withdrawn from sale, his name was removed from theatre posters and he was declared bankrupt. Wilde had been ostracised. On his release, he was philosophical about his time in prison. It had given him time to study himself and there had certainly been long periods of soul-searching – 'that might bring balm to the bruised heart, and peace to the soul in pain', he wrote to Lord Alfred Douglas.

Each Man Kills the Thing He Loves

While in prison, Wilde wrote The Ballad of Reading Gaol (published in 1898), about a man hanged there for the murder of his wife. The execution cast a long shadow over the inmates, and Wilde in particular, but this work, more than any other, gave him status as a writer of serious merit.

WALK 36 DIRECTIONS

❶ Start by the statue of Queen Victoria and, with your back to the Town Hall, turn right, pass the tourist information centre and the museum. Cross Valpy Street and turn right into Forbury Road. Walk down to the roundabout, where the Rising Sun pub is seen on the corner, and turn left towards the railway bridge. Pass beneath the line and cross the road at the pedestrian lights. Avoid King's Meadow Road and make for Reading Bridge.

❷ Take the steps on the right just before the bridge and join the Thames Path, heading downstream with the river on your left. Pass Caversham Lock as the sound of traffic begins to fade and the surroundings become

WALK 36

leafier. Skirt King's Meadow, with smart apartment buildings and lines of houses on the opposite bank. Pass a boat yard, full of cabin cruisers and narrow boats, and continue under the branches of horse chestnut trees. Eventually reach Kennet Mouth and here a distinctive Sustrans waymark directs you over the bridge (in the direction of Bristol!).

WHILE YOU'RE THERE

Visit the Museum of Reading, next door to the tourist information centre. Here you can see a full-size replica of the Bayeux Tapestry, discover artefacts from the Roman town of Silchester and learn about the history of Huntley and Palmers, Reading's famous biscuit factory.

3 Cross Horseshoe Bridge and turn left on the far side, heading for central Reading. Pass beneath Brunel's railway bridge, continue to The Fisherman's Cottage and Blakes Lock, and leave the canal tow path at the next bridge. Turn right along King's Road, passing the wonderful listed façade of the Huntley and Palmer's biscuit factory, then turn immediately right and cross the bridge built by the Reading Gas Company in 1880. Join the tow path and keep the vast hulk of the Prudential building over on the left bank.

WHERE TO EAT AND DRINK

Reading offers numerous pubs, café bars, restaurants and hotels. However, on the walk itself you might like to stop off at The Fisherman's Cottage, which overlooks the Kennet and Avon Canal, and enjoy a meal or snack in the pub's conservatory, which has a striking riverside mural. Alternatively, sit outside on a sunny day and enjoy the canal scene. Fresh bread is available daily and there are baguettes to take away.

4 Pass under King's Road, keep to the right and follow Chestnut Walk, since 2000 also known as the Oscar Wilde Memorial Walk. Reading Gaol, where Oscar Wilde was imprisoned, can be seen over to the right. Walk along to the ruins of Reading Abbey and turn right. Keep alongside the impressive abbey ruins and enter Forbury Gardens through a flint arch. Keep to the left edge, with the statue of the lion, erected to commemorate the 19th-century imperial campaigns in Afghanistan, on your right. Look for the abbey gateway on the left, with Reading Crown Court adjacent, and exit at Victoria Gate. Walk ahead to the The Forbury, pass the Church of St Laurence-in-Reading on the right and return to the tourist information centre and the statue at the start of the walk.

WHAT TO LOOK OUT FOR

Horseshoe Bridge is where the Kennet and the Thames meet. Earley Wharf once stood on this site – and it may have been used by the Romans to serve their local town of Silchester, on the Berkshire/Hampshire border. Threatened by several road schemes over the years, Kennet Mouth and the bridge were saved by a campaign fought by those who value this historic corner of Reading. Reading Abbey was established by Henry I and its history is recorded on the wall outside. Henry VIII sealed its fate with the Dissolution of the Monasteries. The last abbot, Hugh Faringdon, protested in the most vigorous terms, was charged with high treason, found guilty and hanged. The buildings were desecrated during the Civil War.

A Fashionable Riverside Resort at Pangbourne

Journey to the peaceful waters of the Pang before heading for the Thames Path and a National Trust meadow.

DISTANCE 3 miles (4.8km)	**MINIMUM TIME** 1hr 30min
ASCENT/GRADIENT 220ft (67m) ▲▲▲	**LEVEL OF DIFFICULTY** +++

PATHS Field and riverside paths, stretches of road, section of Thames Path, 2 stiles

LANDSCAPE Gentle farmland on banks of Pang and Thames

SUGGESTED MAP OS Explorer 159 Reading, Wokingham & Pangbourne

START/FINISH Grid reference: SU 633765

DOG FRIENDLINESS On lead in Pangbourne, under control on farmland and by River Thames

PARKING Car park off A329 in Pangbourne, near railway bridge

PUBLIC TOILETS At car park

During the Edwardian era the Thames-side settlement of Pangbourne became especially fashionable with artists, writers and anglers, yet apparently it did little to ignite the interest of one renowned literary figure. 'Pleasant house, hate Pangbourne, nothing happens', wrote D H Lawrence (see Walk 42) in 1919 when he and his wife rented a cottage in the village.

Popular Pangbourne

On the other hand, D H Evans, who founded the famous West End department store, clearly found Pangbourne to his liking. Towards the end of the 19th century he built seven very distinctive villas in the village. Known as the Seven Deadly Sins and distinguished by domes, turrets, balconies and gables, the villas were not popular with everyone.

There were those who claimed the seven villas had been built to house Evans' seven mistresses, while others believed he lived in a different one each day of the week. Lady Cunard, noted for her notorious parties, bought one of the houses. One local resident claimed the parties were riotous and wild, adding 'anything would have seemed wild compared to life in Pangbourne'.

Without the river, Pangbourne would hardly have gained its reputation as an inland resort. The spacious meadows, glorious hanging woods and varied assortment of pubs and hotels have made the village one of the most popular destinations on this stretch of the Thames. One man whose love for this river lasted a lifetime was Kenneth Grahame. He wrote *The Wind in the Willows* in 1908 and found the inspiration for this delightful story here. Grahame was born in 1859 and first came to live in Berkshire when he was five. His strength lay in his ability to create a magical world for children, providing a fascinating insight into a child's imagination and their view of the puzzling adult world.

Grahame and his wife became parents rather late in life and it was their son's bedtime stories, as well as letters sent to the boy by his father while away on holiday, that formed the basis for Grahame's classic *The Wind in the Willows*. Both father and son drew on their love of the Berkshire countryside and its wild creatures to complete the story. Having lived for much of his life in the Thames Valley, Grahame eventually moved to Pangbourne in 1924, buying Church Cottage in the centre of the village. His beloved Thames was only a short walk away and he died here in 1932.

WALK 37 DIRECTIONS

1 From the car park turn right to the mini-roundabout and walk along to the church and adjoining Church Cottage. Retrace your steps to the main road, keep the Cross Keys pub on the right and turn right at the mini-roundabout. Cross the Pang and bear right at the next major junction into The Moors. At the end of the drive continue ahead on a waymarked

footpath. Pass alongside various houses and gardens and patches of scrub, then go through a pretty tunnel of trees. Further on is a gate with a local map and an information board about the area. Beyond the gate the River Pang can be seen sweeping in from the right.

2 Follow the riverside path, with white willow trees seen on the bank. Make for a footbridge.

PANGBOURNE

WALK 37

gate turn right at the next bridge and follow the concrete track as it bends left to run beneath the railway line. Once through it, bear right to a kissing gate and then follow the track along the left edge of the field, beside a rivulet. Ahead on the horizon are glorious hanging woods on the north bank of the Thames. Pass double galvanised gates and a bridge on the left and continue on the footpath as it crosses this gentle lowland landscape. Go through a kissing gate and walk across the next field to reach the river bank.

Don't cross it, instead, turn sharp left and walk across the open meadow to a kissing gate in the far boundary. Once over it, keep alongside the hedge on the left and, as you approach a Second World War pill box, turn right at a path intersection and cross a footbridge. Head for another footbridge on the far side of the field and then look for a third bridge with white railings, by the field boundary. Cross the bridge and the stile beyond it and then head across the field to the far boundary.

❸ Exit to the road and bear left. Follow the lane between hedges and oak trees and walk along to the A329. Go diagonally right to the footpath by the sign for Purley Rise and follow the path north towards distant trees, a steam on your left. Through a kissing

❹ On reaching the River Thames, turn left through a kissing gate and over a footbridge and head towards Pangbourne. Follow the Thames Path to Pangbourne Meadow and up ahead now is Whitchurch Bridge. As you approach it, begin to veer away from the river bank towards a car park. Keep left when you get to the road, pass beneath the railway line and turn right at the next junction. Bear right again at the mini-roundabout and return to the car park.

Overleaf: The River Pang at Pangbourne

Frilsham and a Classic Country Pub

On a warm summer's day, this delightful woodland walk offers plenty of welcome shade.

DISTANCE 3.5 miles (5.7km)   MINIMUM TIME 1hr 30min

ASCENT/GRADIENT 99ft (30m) ▲▲▲   LEVEL OF DIFFICULTY +++

PATHS Tracks, paths and stretches of country road, no stiles

LANDSCAPE Woodland on northern side of Pang Valley

SUGGESTED MAP OS Explorer 158 Newbury & Hungerford

START/FINISH Grid reference: SU 552730

DOG FRIENDLINESS Under control on Yattendon Estate

PARKING Space at side of Pot Kiln

PUBLIC TOILETS None en route

Sadly, in some English pubs the familiar call 'time Gentlemen please' has assumed a new significance. It isn't just the deregulation of licensing laws that threatens to make this age-old cry redundant, but the continued existence of the traditional public house. One of England's greatest institutions has been under threat for some time, and yet it remains an integral part of rural and urban life.

The Birth of the English Pub

Our pubs are unique to this country but how exactly did they begin? The story of the English pub spans more than 1,000 years of history, beginning with the dismal alehouses of the Anglo-Saxon period. Later came the old drovers' hostelries, followed by coaching inns and then Georgian and Victorian pubs built to take advantage of the canal and railway trade. Finally, today, we have the familiar theme boozer and the up-market restaurant establishment, neither of which bear much resemblance to the traditional image of the genuine, authentic local.

Preserving Tradition

It's hard to find a pub that hasn't been altered in one way or another. Many have gone altogether, while others have made subtle changes to meet modern demands. And those that appear not to have changed in any way have almost certainly been very clever and tapped into a niche market. Preserving a pub by retaining its antique tills and fading wallpaper, giving the impression it belongs in some sort of fossilised time warp like a museum piece, often produces dividends. The landlord may deliberately chose not to move with the times, knowing that the look, feel and atmosphere of his pub conveys the right impression and that it is what many people want.

Traditional Local

One such pub belonging in this particular category is The Pot Kiln, a famous tavern in an isolated part of Berkshire. Until the beginning of the Second World War, there were brick kilns in this area – hence the name of the pub. Hidden among trees, The Pot Kiln is superbly located down a narrow country lane and is quite hard to find. There have been many additions and various changes to the inn over the years, but, thankfully, The Pot Kiln retains its original character. Many of its supporters feel it should have a protection order slapped on it, so that it stand as a permanent reminder of how country pubs used to be.

From the outside, the inn could almost pass for a farm or a private house. Inside are two bars – lounge and public – and between them is an off-sales hatch in the panelled lobby. The lounge bar has tables and bar stools, bench seats and a log fire in winter.

FRILSHAM

WALK 38 DIRECTIONS

1 Go to the end of the car park at the side of The Pot Kiln and follow the track. Keep the microbrewery on your left and pass several houses, including Laurel Bank Cottages. Avoid a public footpath on the left and continue to two cottages at right angles to the byway. Bear left just beyond them and follow a footpath between holly trees. Disregard the turning on the left and, noting St Frideswide's Well to the left, keep right at the next fork. Head for the road and turn left. Walk through Frilsham village, pass Beechfield, a residential development, and turn left at the sign for Hermitage and Bucklebury.

2 Beyond Little Orchard, when the lane bends right, go straight ahead, following the path deep into the woods. Pass through a gate and continue on the bridleway to the next waymark. Branch off to the left at this point, following the path down the wooded slope to the road. Cross over and continue ahead on the track, signed 'Restricted Byway'. Piles of logs can often be seen lining the route, waiting to be transported to the sawmills. Pass a waymarked track on the right and continue on the main track, following it through ornamental woodland to the next waymarked junction.

3 Bear left here and cut through bluebell woods to a gate. Cross the field to a fence gap in the next boundary, with traffic on the M4 visible in the distance. Veer half left in the field and away to the right in the distance, you can just make out the façade of Yattendon Court, up among the trees. Cross the field and make for a bridleway gate on the right, running into the trees.

4 Beyond the wood, follow the path between fences and swing left at the next waymarked junction. Walk along the track to the next junction, where there are footpath and bridleway signs, and veer right. Follow the track round the side of Magpie Farm and on reaching the road, turn left. Return to the car park by The Pot Kiln.

The Bull at Stanford Dingley

Follow pretty woodland paths down into the Pang Valley.

See map and information panel for Walk 38

DISTANCE 8 miles (12.9km) **MINIMUM TIME** 3hrs 45min
ASCENT/GRADIENT 95ft (29m) ▲▲▲ **LEVEL OF DIFFICULTY** +++

WALK 39 DIRECTIONS
(Walk 38 option)

After crossing the lane between Points ❷ and ❸ in Walk 38, follow the track and turn right on to another track at the waymarked junction, Point Ⓐ. Go straight on at the next waymark and eventually reach a drive by a house. Walk down a lane to the road and bear right. Turn left at the next junction, towards Bucklebury. Cross the Pang and go straight ahead, through a kissing gate and across the field to the church via another, Point Ⓑ.

Leave the church, keep left and head towards a timber-framed cottage. Exit to the road and turn left. Take the next left-hand right of way, opposite the former School House. Follow a grassy track and three-quarters of the way across a field, reach the corner of a ditch and a waymark. Turn left and head for a footbridge and stile. Continue ahead in the next field and make for a bridge, crossing it. Turn right to follow the Pang to Stanford Dingley.

Go through a ruined gate then keep ahead on a waterside path, eventually reaching two stiles, a gate and a track. Bear right here for about 80yds (73m) to the next gateway, swinging left immediately before it. Keep left

as the path forks, making for a kissing gate among the trees in the far corner. Cross a footbridge and go through a wood to the next kissing gate and then follow the path across the pasture, keeping Stanford Dingley church in view. Make for a stile at the road and turn right to visit the Bull, Point Ⓒ, another classic pub.

This village inn dates back to the 15th century and includes a wealth of original timbers as well as the remains of an original wattle and daub wall. One of its more unusual features is the traditional, and now quite rare, pub game known as ring-the-bull, involving a genuine surviving bull's ring.

To continue the walk, keep left past the church and head away from the village. Take the first left turning, signposted 'Bucklebury'. As the road begins to curve left, look for a path and stile on the right and enter the field. Follow the boundary to a stile and walk ahead across the next field, aiming to the right of Pangfield Farm. As you draw level with the outbuildings, take the permissive path on the right. Join the right of way further along and follow it between trees and then through the woodland. Keep ahead to the next waymarked junction and rejoin Walk 38 at Point ❸.

In Praise of Douai

*Enjoy a quiet country walk and visit a magnificent
newly built abbey church.*

DISTANCE *3 miles (4.8km)* MINIMUM TIME *1hr 30min*

ASCENT/GRADIENT *90ft (27m)* ▲▲▲ LEVEL OF DIFFICULTY +++

PATHS *Tracks, field and woodland paths, stretches of
village road and country lane, 2 stiles*

LANDSCAPE *Mixture of woodland and farmland
on south-facing slopes of Kennet Valley*

SUGGESTED MAP *OS Explorer 159 Reading, Wokingham & Pangbourne*

START/FINISH *Grid reference: SU 589688*

DOG FRIENDLINESS *On lead in Beenham, near Douai and near livestock,
under control on woodland stretches*

PARKING *Small car park by Victory Hall*

PUBLIC TOILETS *None en route*

WALK 40 DIRECTIONS

From the car park turn right and
follow the road through Beenham
to Clay Lane. Veer left and left
again by Jayswood Cottage. Follow
the byway and pass the entrance
to Oakwood Farm. When the
track curves left, swing right at
the bridleway sign. Cross a stream
and a stile to walk uphill beside a
hedge to a gate. Continue ahead
and then skirt Malthouse Farm via
two gates, a stile and across to a
third gate at the road.

Turn right and head up the road
towards Douai Abbey and look

for a footpath on the left, leading
across the playing field to St Peter's
Church at Woolhampton. Keep
to the left of the pavilion and
look for the kissing gate into the
churchyard. Turn right at the road,
pass the school and follow the road
round the right bend. At the main
entrance to Douai Abbey, bear left
by some thatched cottages and pass
the abbey church.

Work on this splendid building
began in 1928 and the east end
was completed in 1933. However,
it was the summer of 1993 before
the church was completed and
dedicated. The original design,
by Arnold Crush, can be seen in
the choir and sanctuary areas. The
initial plan was to have a transept
crossing surmounted by a tower,
and, with another seven bays,
the church would have extended
almost to the road.

When, years after work began,
circumstances eventually allowed
its completion, the monastic

WHERE TO EAT AND DRINK

The Six Bells at Beenham is
ideally placed, right in the
centre of Beenham. Try one of
the snacks, perhaps soup and a
baguette, or for something more
substantial there are such dishes
as steak and kidney pudding,
lasagne and a range of omelettes.

DOUAI

community at Douai chose to finish the church in a style that suited the modern age, with the focus on prayer and praise. In 1987 Dr Michael Blee was invited to start work on a new design.

Step inside and you'll spot several notable memorials. One is to pupils of the former school killed in the world wars, while another commemorates all those who contributed to the building of the new church. The chapel to the north was originally dedicated to St Benedict and is now the Blessed Sacrament Chapel, used for private prayer and worship.

The church may be new but what of Douai's history? The abbey community covers more than three and a half centuries. The Dissolution of the Monasteries during the reign of Henry VIII drove men and women who opted for a monastic existence to flee abroad. In 1615 a group of English

monks gathered in Paris to form the community of St Edmund. Other English monasteries were formed and together they restored the English Benedictine Congregation.

Having been suppressed and almost extinguished by the events of the French Revolution, the survivors of St Edmund's moved, in 1818, to Douai in France. In 1903 the monks were again expelled from their monastery on anti-clerical grounds. This time they crossed the channel to Berkshire, taking the name 'Douai' with them. They took over the existing St Mary's College, transforming it into a leading Roman Catholic public school for boys, which closed in 1999.

These days the Douai community includes around 30 monks, who receive guests here, host conferences and offer a place of retreat. They also help organise events in the church itself and in other parts of the abbey campus, as well as working in the surrounding parish.

Beyond the church, continue along the road to some cottages and barns. Turn right at a footpath sign, soon passing a galvanised gate, and follow the track into the next field. Keep to the field-edge and when you reach the corner, by the footpath sign, go straight over into the woods. Fields can be seen close by on the left. Follow the path through the trees then between paddocks and eventually reach the outskirts of Beenham.

Turn left at the junction, then right by Jayswood Cottage, back into the centre of the village. The Six Bells pub is on the left and the car park, where the walk began, is near by.

Enduring Brimpton

*A walk through Wasing Park to Brimpton
overlooking the Kennet Valley.*

DISTANCE 6.5 miles (10.4km)	**MINIMUM TIME** 2hrs 45min

ASCENT/GRADIENT 150ft (46m) ▲▲▲ **LEVEL OF DIFFICULTY** +++

PATHS Field and woodland paths and tracks, parkland drives, meadow, road and riverside, 11 stiles

LANDSCAPE Common, parkland, woodland and meadow

SUGGESTED MAP OS Explorer 159 Reading, Wokingham & Pangbourne

START/FINISH Grid reference: SU 567628

DOG FRIENDLINESS On lead in Wasing Park and Ashford Hill Meadows

PARKING Limited spaces in lay-by opposite The Pineapple pub

PUBLIC TOILETS None en route

The English village is one of the key elements that have helped to shape the rural character of this country over the centuries. England's village communities are etched into the fabric of its society, reflecting a way of life that is the envy of others.

Typical Village

However, there is concern that some time-honoured traditions are being eroded. The village is such a vital and integral part of our rural landscape that, despite the tide of social change in the country, it is likely to survive – though, almost certainly, in a different form.

Berkshire, like Buckinghamshire, is blessed with many fine villages that, thankfully, have stood the test of time and remained largely intact. Some have fallen victim to planning blight and seen their boundaries expanded in recent years, while others have successfully fought off late 20th-century development, their pride and spirit intact.

One such village that has so far avoided change is Brimpton, just to the south of the A4, between Newbury and Reading. Bounded to the north by the River Kennet and to the south by the lesser-known Enborne, Brimpton, in the main, lies at the end of a breezy ridge. As a village, it's like hundreds of others around the country. But it is that similarity that makes it a typical English rural community. Look closely and you'll see that its key component parts remain in place – the shop and post office, the public house, the primary school and the church are all here.

Village records reveal a fascinating insight into how Brimpton has evolved over the years into the community you see today. As with most rural settlements, Brimpton was once part of the feudal system, shaped and controlled by landowning families, aristocrats and local benefactors. In 1854 the Countess of Falmouth built almshouses for elderly couples and widows, while the Earl donated a small piece of land on which to build a school. Later, when the church was rebuilt, the local squire, James Blyth, objected to the pub being near the church and gave land for a new site.

BRIMPTON

The local shop was once the home of Duncan McClean, who moved here in 1920. Blinded in the First World War, McClean was a basket and net maker, as well as a poultry farmer; his wife established the village stores. Nearby Glebe Cottage was once The Brimpton Refreshment Rooms. Brimpton's villagers unveiled an illustrated map of the village and its history outside the church to mark the new millennium.

WALK 41 DIRECTIONS

1 Follow the path opposite The Pineapple across two stiles to the road. Cross over to join a byway, follow it round to the right and across the common. When it swings sharp left, go straight on along the public footpath, still a track. Take the path to the right of Woodside, bear left at a T-junction and follow the path. Where it joins a track, veer off left at a waymark, following the field-edge path. Look for an opening in the trees ahead, cross a bridge and turn right at a track. At a track junction go right, following it to a sign for Wasing Church. If you reach a tarmac lane you have missed the right turn.

❷ Pass the gate, take the track, turn left at the bend and cut through the wood. Cross a track through a kissing gate, then a field to visit the church via another kissing gate, then return to the drive. Turn right and pass between gate piers and continue ahead at crossroads over cattle grid to follow the drive down to the road beyond a gate and a lodge. Bear left to a junction, then right over the Enborne to a fork. Keep left on to Wasing Road and turn right at the Wasing Estate sign. Through a gate veer left along a grassy track to a junction and bear left by a galvanised gate.

❸ Follow the path to the road, turn right for several paces, then left to join the next path through a kissing gate. Keep over to the left edge of the field, go through a kissing gate in the top corner and veer right. Turn right through a kissing gate to reach a housing estate. Bear right at the road and walk along to the church,

following the path beside it. On reaching a field corner, go straight on, swinging left by second set of power lines. Head south to Hyde End Lane via three gates.

❹ Turn left, keeping right at the fork on to a stony track, passing Hyde End House entrance. Look for a stile to the left of a footbridge and cross a meadow. Over stile, follow the river bank to a footbridge and stile. Cross over and take the path through wood to a brick bridge. Cross the road and follow the track, taking the path to the left of it between the woodland edge and wire fence and, over stile and plank bridge, make for a bridge in the far right corner of the field. Follow a line of trees to a stile and cross the next pasture towards buildings. Approaching a gate and a cottage, veer left to a stile. Cross to another stile by the road.

❺ Turn right over the bridge and bear left to a kissing gate leading into Ashford Hill Meadows, veering left across pastures. After 75yds (69m), look closely for a fork and branch off left to a footbridge. Begin crossing a field and after about 120yds (110m), make for a footbridge and gate on the left. Through the gate continue ahead to two oaks in the left hedge which conceals a kissing gate. Through this turn right along a narrow field to a kissing gate at the edge of the woods. Follow the path up through the trees, merging with a track from the right. Over a stile at the edge of the woods, turn half left and cross the field to the next stile. Go straight ahead along a lane and when it bends right, bear left and follow the path to the road. Continue ahead, returning to the lay-by by the pub.

Hermitage – a Writer's Wartime Refuge

Explore dense woodland and pass the former home of a famous British novelist on this spectacular walk near Newbury.

DISTANCE *6 miles (9.7km)*   MINIMUM TIME *2hrs 45min*

ASCENT/GRADIENT *320ft (98m)* ▲▲▲   LEVEL OF DIFFICULTY +++

PATHS *Field and woodland paths and tracks, some road, 6 stiles*

LANDSCAPE *Extensive woodland with areas of open farmland*

SUGGESTED MAP *OS Explorer 158 Newbury & Hungerford*

START/FINISH *Grid reference: SU 505730*

DOG FRIENDLINESS *Under control in woods and on lead near livestock*

PARKING *Limited parking in Hermitage*

PUBLIC TOILETS *None en route*

It is a little-known fact that one of Britain's most famous and outspoken 20th-century writers lived quietly in a Berkshire village at the end of the First World War. What is even more surprising is that he and his wife deliberately chose a low profile. But why?

D H Lawrence

During the early years of the First World War David Herbert Lawrence (1885–1930) and his German bride Frieda lived near St Ives in Cornwall, but were not accepted by the local community. In remote rural areas, women such as Lawrence's wife were often looked upon with suspicion and hatred. The war had been long and bloody and Frieda, living among people who had lost loved ones, was an unwelcome reminder of Germany's part in it. In one among several letters, Lawrence wrote: 'Sudden blow! We are served with notice to leave the area of Cornwall by Monday next... by the military. It is a complete mystery to me – complete.'

Move to Berkshire

Forced to leave Cornwall, the couple moved to Hermitage near Newbury in December 1917, renting a small cottage from a friend. It was a quiet and peaceful place but even here Lawrence and his wife were not left alone. While living at Chapel Farm Cottage, they received regular calls from the police. To make matters worse, Lawrence was a pacifist and openly opposed the war. Ill health gave him a genuine reason not to fight, but his outspoken views and choice of bride did not endear him to the villagers.

Walking All Day

However, Lawrence liked life in Berkshire and would walk many miles in a day. He was able to combine his knowledge of the countryside with his skill as a writer, using prose and imagery to convey his love of creation. A keen artist and gardener, Lawrence would also write at great speed and it was while living at Chapel Farm Cottage that he undertook some revision of earlier work, including *Women in Love* (1921).

HERMITAGE

Prolific Writer

During the two years he lived at the cottage, Lawrence worked on various short stories, several novels and some poetry. Of all his writing, the story most closely associated with Hermitage is The Fox, first published in 1923 in *Three Novellas*. The story is set at Bailey Farm, which Lawrence based on Grimsbury Farm, just outside the village. The setting for the farm, the surrounding countryside and the nearby railway are all faithfully recreated in The Fox, while the nearby market town is undoubtedly Newbury. Lawrence left Hermitage for Italy in November 1919.

WALK 42 DIRECTIONS

1 From the village hall in Hermitage turn right, then right again into Doctors Lane. Cross a stile by a private road sign and head across the field to the next stile. Pass beneath power lines and make for a stile in the boundary of the woodland ahead of you. Over the stile, soon take the left fork and follow the footpath through the trees as far as a cottage. Turn left when you reach the track and veer right after about 100yds (91m) at the public footpath sign. Drop down through the woodland to a lane and keep to the right. Walk along the lane to the hamlet of Oare and turn right by a small pond. Over a stile continue alongside a hedge.

2 Head towards the buildings of Little Hungerford, cross a stile and turn right at the road. Bear left into Chapel Lane and follow the road round the right-hand bend. Pass Pond Lane and D H Lawrence's former home on the corner as you head for the next road junction. Chapel Farm Cottage is clearly identified – its front entrance is in Pond Lane and its rear garden backs on to Chapel Lane. At the main road turn

left and walk along to a public footpath sign on the right. Over a stile follow the track deep into Box Wood and eventually reach a waymarked junction.

3 Bear right here on to a restricted byway and follow the track through the trees to the next road. Cross over by a bungalow and continue on the next section of track. Turn right at the next road and walk along to the turning for Boar's Hole Farm on the left. Follow the track to the farm and continue south to a sharp left-hand bend. Go through the gate on the right and make for a gate and house in the field corner. Keep to the right of the house via a gate and turn right at a track bend and crossroads, passing through a galvanised metal gate on to a restricted byway.

4 Follow the woodland track and keep right at the fork. Cross a stream and pass a left turning. Take the next left path by a stream and pass over a staggered junction. Turn right by the pond, then first left, cutting through the trees. Swing right at the next junction and follow the track as it eventually runs up by a (currently damaged) seat. Now within Grimsbury Castle's ramparts, keep left at the junction and make for the road by a cottage. Opposite are the earthworks of Grimsbury Castle. Turn right and walk along to the road junction. Bear left and return to Hermitage.

Donnington Castle – a Civil War Stronghold

Stroll through a country park to a castle overlooking the Kennet Valley.

DISTANCE *3.5 miles (5.7km)*	MINIMUM TIME *1hr 45min*

ASCENT/GRADIENT *165ft (50m)* ▲▲▲   LEVEL OF DIFFICULTY ✦✦✦

PATHS *Paths and tracks through woods*

LANDSCAPE *Formal country park, golf course and woodland*

SUGGESTED MAP *OS Explorer 158 Newbury & Hungerford*

START/FINISH *Grid reference: SU 463709*

DOG FRIENDLINESS *Under control at Snelsmore Common and by golf course*

PARKING *Car park at Snelsmore Common Country Park*

PUBLIC TOILETS *Snelsmore Common Country Park*

On a hillside to the north of Newbury lie the remains of Donnington Castle, once a major stronghold commanding the key routes through the town – now the A4 and the A34. The castle's strategic importance was immense and was borne out by the prolonged fighting for it during the Civil War. Today, what remains of Donnington Castle looks down forlornly on a town that has spready widely since those days.

A Long History

The manor of Deritone (now Donnington) was held by the Crown in 1086. In 1386 Richard II granted a licence to 'build anew' and crenellate Donnington Castle, to Sir Richard de Abberbury, a former guardian of the King. Later, the castle passed to Thomas Chaucer, probably the son of the poet. By the time of Elizabeth I it was back in royal possession – there are accounts of the restoration work to the castle in preparation for her visit there in 1568. This included planking the bridge, mending chamber floors, building sheds for the kitchen and making tables, forms and trestles.

Civil War

At the time of the Civil War, Donnington Castle belonged to John Packer, whose refusal of a loan to the King and opposition in Parliament led to the sequestration of his property by Charles I. Colonel John Boys was sent to take command of the castle for the King in 1643, with 200 foot soldiers, 25 horses and four pieces of cannon. He strengthened the defences by constructing the star fort earthworks around it, which can still be seen below the castle. Boys withstood two Parliamentary assaults on the castle in July and September 1644 and was knighted by the King in October.

The Second Battle of Newbury, on 27 October 1644, was somewhat inconclusive, but the Royalist Army was able to slip away leaving the Crown, Great Seal and artillery in Boys' keeping at Donnington. Boys then withstood another siege by the Parliamentary army until relieved by the King on 9 November. Repeated attempts were made to take the castle, but Boys did not surrender until instructed to do so by the King

DONNINGTON CASTLE

on 1 April, 1646. The outline of the castle can be seen today but the most impressive feature still standing is its magnificent gatehouse. The grounds of Donnington Castle are open every day of the week and on most weekends there are at least a handful of people surveying the ruins and gazing out across Newbury to the hills and downland beyond.

WALK 43 DIRECTIONS

1 Keep the toilet block on your right and walk ahead to a vehicle barrier and a sign for the country park. Veer right at the fork and

pass between sunny glades and picnic tables and benches. Follow the track to a kissing gate. Beyond them the track curves gradually to the left and then runs clear and straight to a left curve. Pass a path on the right here and continue for a few paces to a bridleway.

❷ Turn sharp right and keep left at the next fork, avoiding a path on the extreme left. Keep to the right of a wooden seat and descend the bank between bracken. Cut through the trees at the bottom to a galvanised gate and follow the path ahead as it upgrades to a track. Pass Chestnut and Honey Bottom Cottages and go straight ahead when the track bends right. Follow the path along the woodland edge, then alongside a golf course until you reach a wooden kissing gate on the right.

❸ Head down the field slope towards Bagnor between fences. Make for a gate and follow the grassy path to the road. Turn left, pass The Blackbird inn and follow the track at the end of the car park. Go through the kissing gate and take the tarmac path up over the A34 to a golf course. Keep

left at the fork on the far side of the footbridge, heading towards woodland and an intersection. Cross the drive and follow a waymarked path on the right, threading through the trees. Keep the greens and fairways on the right. Emerge from the woodland at a gate and climb the slope to Donnington Castle.

❹ Look for a gate behind it, leading to a track, and turn left. Pass between the timber barns of Castle Farm and bear left, down the tarmac bridleway. Re-cross the bypass and sweep right along the bridleway, following the drive as it dwindles to a track. Keep right at the fork and cut between fences. On the left are extensive fairways. Follow the track towards a house set against the trees and keep to the left of it, staying on the bridleway.

❺ Pass through a gate on to Snelsmore Common and go straight ahead at the waymarked junction. Pass beneath power lines and continue between bracken and gorse bushes. Keep right at the next fork and follow the waymark pointing towards the car park. A useful directional landmark is the fire control tower, seen on this stretch. Merge with another path at the next waymark and, within sight of the road and just before a stile, look for a galvanised gate on the left. Go through it and return to the car park.

Setting the Stage at Bagnor

An attractive extra loop on the delightful Lambourn Valley Way.
See map and information panel for Walk 43

DISTANCE *3 miles (4.8km)* MINIMUM TIME *1hr 30min*
ASCENT/GRADIENT *82ft (25m)* ▲▲▲ LEVEL OF DIFFICULTY +++

WALK 44 DIRECTIONS
(Walk 43 option)

On reaching Bagnor (Point ③ on Walk 43), turn right along the main street, cross the River Lambourn and pass the entrance to the Watermill Theatre, the West Berkshire Playhouse. A short walk along the drive reveals a striking view of the mill. This dates back to 1839 and was used to produce good quality writing paper before becoming a corn mill in the 1850s. The Watermill Theatre, which opened in 1965, has staged many prestigious productions over the years, earning well-deserved praise and plaudits from the arts world.

Continue along the road and take the next turning on the left. Follow the drive, part of the Lambourn Valley Way, and keep right at the entrance to Bagnor Manor. Pass a traffic mirror on the left and a bridleway on the right, over a stile, and continue ahead to another stile, Point Ⓐ.

Don't cross it, instead swing right and follow the way between hedgerows. Further on, the track curves gently to the right by a grove of trees.

Eventually pass a stile on the right before the trail runs between trees. As you emerge from the woodland, swing left at the waymark and follow the path down to a stile and a bridge spanning the Lambourn. Cross over and veer right, taking the path by the meadow. Cross a weir and bridge to a stile and make for the dismantled Lambourn Valley railway. Make for another stile and go out to the road, Point Ⓑ.

Cross over and follow the byway ahead, keeping to the right of Priddle's Farm. After it bends left, pass the entrance to Woodspeen Farm and continue to the road on a bend at Rookwood. Swing left at this point to join a byway, following the muddy sunken path as it descends to Snake Lane. Bear left and walk to the road junction. Cross over and follow the waymarked lane, swinging right to a footbridge when you reach Crossways Cottage, Point Ⓒ.

Follow the riverside path. Cross two bridges to a stile and continue between fields and fences to the next stile. Continue ahead along the concrete drive and retrace your steps to the centre of Bagnor, rejoining Walk 43.

War and Peace at Greenham

Walk along a canal to a notorious common,
returning to the start by train.

DISTANCE 6.5 miles (10.4km)	MINIMUM TIME 2hrs 30min

ASCENT/GRADIENT Negligible ▲▲▲   LEVEL OF DIFFICULTY +++

PATHS Canal tow path, tracks, common paths, roads, 1 stile

LANDSCAPE Valley rising to wooded commons

SUGGESTED MAP OS Explorer 158 Newbury & Hungerford

START / FINISH Grid reference: SU 527663

DOG FRIENDLINESS On lead at Crookham and Greenham commons during breeding season, under control on canal tow path

PARKING Thatcham Station

PUBLIC TOILETS Newbury town and station

WALK 45 DIRECTIONS

From Thatcham Station make for the Kennet and Avon Canal, a few paces to the south of the barrier, and turn right, signposted 'Ham Bridge'. Pass Monkey Marsh Lock and at the swing bridge, by a bridleway sign, turn left to Chamberhouse Farm. Pass between the sprawling farm outbuildings and follow the drive past the farmhouse and several cottages. The density of the buildings somehow conveys the impression that you are walking along the main street of a small village.

Cross the River Kennet and just beyond it the drive curves left. Keep right here and follow the track as it runs up through woodland to the road. Cross over to a gate leading on to Crookham Common and turn right. Follow the path parallel to the road, heading west. The television mast at Hannington and the ridge of Watership Down define the horizon.

Greenham Common's former airbase was once synonymous with CND rallies, women's protest groups and cruise missiles – a powerful evocation of the Cold War period and the threat of nuclear attack. Today, the derelict buildings have been demolished and the perimeter fence has been removed.

Originally an area of open common land, Greenham was acquired by the Air Ministry in 1941 for use as a military base, home to British squadrons and then the United States Air Force. In 1951 the Americans set about building the longest military runway in Europe here and in the early 1980s the nuclear-

WHILE YOU'RE THERE

If you've got the time, take a stroll through Newbury itself. There's plenty to see, including the West Berkshire Museum, housed in the 17th-century Cloth Hall, built to provide unemployed weavers with work.

armed cruise missiles arrived, making Greenham Common a focus of world attention. In its day, the airbase was virtually a self-contained American city, with everything from baseball pitches to its own school. The 1,000 acre (405ha) site even hosted international air shows and some local people feared that it might become the new London airport. Today the only sound you are likely to hear is that of birdsong. Thanks to a £7 million package, Greenham Common is at last being restored to its pre-Second World War state.

Follow the stony path which winds to join the former taxiway, now a popular walk, and eventually pass a hewn log at the side of the path, carved and sculpted to provide three welcome seats. When level with the disused control tower, branch off to the right and go through a gate on the left, leading into the main car park, passing the control tower on your right. Veer right across the car park to a field gate and gate. Soon pass through another gate. Beyond the fence corner bear left at waymark post. At hedge gap go left to a fence, then right and after 40 paces go left through a gate. Descend to a road, cross it and head down through the trees into Bowdown Woods, a nature reserve.

Pass Bowdown Farm and the fairways of Newbury and Crookham Golf Course. Beyond

the greens the chutes and conveyor belts of Lower Farm Quarry loom into view. Continue on the lane to a stile and gate and keep ahead, passing alongside the buildings of Lower Farm. Newbury Racecourse adjoins the route now, its striking grandstand can be seen in the distance. Pass under the railway and look for a swing bridge on the right, crossing the Kennet and Avon Canal. Once across, turn left and follow the tow path as far as Ham Bridge.

Cross and follow the path along the south bank of the Kennet and Avon, making for Ham Lock at the confluence of the Kennet and the River Lambourn. Continue on a leafy stretch of tow path and cross over at the next footbridge, within sight of The Narrow Boat pub. Keep to the path and cross the next bridge at the entrance to the marina. Pass Greenham Lock and walk ahead to the ring road. Pass under the road through a kissing gate and alongside Victoria Park before reaching the next bridge. Leave the tow path, cross the canal into the wharf and keep right past the West Berkshire Museum and continue to the Market Place. Bear left and head south, following Cheap Street to its right-hand bend. Continue ahead a passing the Baptist Church and then go round to the right for the railway station and a train back to Thatcham.

Farnborough's Old Rectory

*Cross breezy downland to the former home of
a fondly remembered poet.*

DISTANCE *7.5 miles (12.1km)* MINIMUM TIME *3hrs*

ASCENT/GRADIENT *150ft (46m)* ▲▲▲ LEVEL OF DIFFICULTY +++

PATHS *Bridleways, field paths, tracks and quiet lanes, 1 stile*

LANDSCAPE *Remote downland country to south of Ridgeway*

SUGGESTED MAP *OS Explorer 170 Abingdon & Wantage*

START/FINISH *Grid reference: SU 471825*

DOG FRIENDLINESS *Under control across farmland*

PARKING *Room to park in West Ilsley's main street*

PUBLIC TOILETS *None en route*

John Betjeman (1906–84) has been described as the most popular poet of the 20th century. With his infectious laugh, air of eccentricity and sense of fun, he was an immensely popular character and, having been born into the television age, he was a natural performer for that particular medium. He loved the camera and it loved him in return.

Home on the Downs

Over the years Betjeman has been the subject of many distinguished television documentaries – intimate portraits that reflected the man's true identity and personality. They demonstrated his love for architecture, for historic landmarks and endangered buildings, illustrating to the viewer how he lovingly brought them to life in his own highly individual style.

However, few of these TV biographies make any mention of his home in the splendid Old Rectory at Farnborough in Berkshire. Betjeman and his wife Penelope moved here in 1945, and in the summer of that year she wrote to a friend: 'Father has bought us a beautiful William and Mary house 700ft up on the downs above Wantage with 12 acres of land, including a wood and two fields. It is a dream of beauty but has no water, no light and is falling down and needs six servants, so it will probably kill us in the end'.

Betjeman spent the war as a press attaché in Dublin, and when it was finally over, he and Penelope returned to their beloved Berkshire. He worked mainly in London, mixing with writers, poets and Oxbridge intellectuals. But he was most at home in the peace and tranquillity of the countryside – especially the Vale of the White Horse, then still within Berkshire. Betjeman loved to explore the downs on foot, while Penelope galloped along the Ridgeway on Moti, her Arab mare.

An Inspiration

The Betjemans' love for this spectacular downland country remained undimmed when they moved to Farnborough. During the six years he lived in the village, Betjeman was typically productive in his work output. His collection of verse *New Bats in Old Belfries* was published in 1945, and in

1948 his *Selected Poems* won the Heinemann Award for Literature. He also worked on *Murray's Architectural Guide for Berkshire*, published in 1949.

The Betjemans moved to Wantage in 1951. It wasn't far away, and here he continued to indulge his love of the English countryside. In a TV interview in 1984, the year he died, Betjeman said that 'poetry makes life worth living', believing that the greatest thing he had done in his own life was to use his eyes and his feelings.

WALK 46 DIRECTIONS

❶ Follow the road out of West Ilsley, heading west. Take the first bridleway on the left and follow track past Starveall Farm uphill to a gate. Continue ahead with the field boundary on your right. Bear left through a gate at the next junction on to ancient track, and then soon right over a stile to follow the path across a large field. Look for a boundary corner ahead and keep ahead in the next field, with the fence on your right. Follow the path across the field to the road, passing a water tower, by Upper Farm, veer left and walk along to Farnborough church and the Old Rectory.

❷ Walk back along the road to the farm, rejoin the track beside the outbuildings and look for a waymark and a pair of galvanised gates after about 60yds (55m). A field footpath and two tracks can be seen here. Keep right, directly alongside the farm. Cut between trees, bushes and margins of vegetation and soon cross a footpath junction. Go further on between dense hedges. Continue ahead to a junction with a byway and bridleway. Keep ahead, going through woodland, following the Ilsley Downs Riding Route. Make for the next junction, where you can see a field beyond the trees, bear right and follow the clear path through the woods.

❸ Keep right at the road and when it bends right, go straight on along a bridleway running across the fields towards trees. At length, the bridleway becomes a byway. Keep ahead when you reach a bend and walk along to a waymarked track on the left. Take it into the woodland and down the slope. As you approach a gap in the hedge, with a field seen ahead, veer right to follow a path running through the trees. Eventually it climbs gently to a junction. The walk turns left, but it is worth

> **WHERE TO EAT AND DRINK**
>
> Overlooking the cricket ground in West Ilsley, the Harrow is a charming village pub. Inside is an attractive open-plan bar offering quality food and imaginatively prepared dishes.

stepping to your right for several paces to admire the timeless view of Woolvers Barn and Woolvers Down.

❹ Follow the byway, avoiding the public footpath on your right, and take the next bridleway on the left. Keep right at the next junction and cut between hedges. When the track bends left, there is a memorable view of West Ilsley sitting snug in its downland setting. Keep right at the next junction, following the track alongside West Ilsley Stables. Cross a cattle grid and turn left along the drive to walk down to the road and turn left. As it bends right by a bridleway sign, go straight on by Keeper's Stables. Swing left as you reach the centre of West Ilsley and pass All Saints Church.

> **WHAT TO LOOK OUT FOR**
>
> Once or twice on this walk, you'll come across voluntary restraint signs, requesting motorists not to indulge in off-road driving. Many cross-country routes have become fragile as a result of this activity.

> **WHILE YOU'RE THERE**
>
> Make a point of looking at the west window in Farnborough's All Saints Church, dedicated to the memory of John Betjeman. The window, which depicts the tree of life, was designed by Betjeman's friend John Piper and executed by Joseph Nuttgens. Have a look at West Ilsley, noted for its horse-racing connections and pretty cottages. Opposite the pub is a striking gazebo, erected by the villagers to mark the new millennium. Look out, too, for the attractively designed parish paths map.

Nags at Chaddleworth

Enjoy an exhilarating walk into
Berkshire's renowned racing country.

DISTANCE *6 miles (9.7km)*   **MINIMUM TIME** *2hrs 30min*

ASCENT/GRADIENT *269ft (82m)* ▲▲▲   **LEVEL OF DIFFICULTY** +++

PATHS *Field paths and tracks, stretches of road, 8 stiles*

LANDSCAPE *Classic farmland and remote, rolling country on edge of Lambourn Downs*

SUGGESTED MAP *OS Explorer 158 Newbury & Hungerford*

START/FINISH *Grid reference: SU 415772*

DOG FRIENDLINESS *On lead near livestock and in region of Whatcombe*

PARKING *Permission given by landlord to park at Ibex pub*

PUBLIC TOILETS *None en route*

The sweeping Lambourn Downs lie at the heart of Berkshire's loveliest and most isolated country – an area with a long tradition for racehorse training. Some of Britain's most famous winners have come from yards at Lambourn and West Ilsley and it is quite common to see strings of horses in the surrounding lanes.

The Sport of Kings

Horse racing dates back to the days of chariot races in Greece and Rome, with blockbuster movies like the immortal *Ben Hur* giving us a flavour of what it would have been like to vie for honours in the mammoth arena. Racing as we know it today has its origins in the period of the Stuart kings. James I established stables at Newmarket and it was here that he kept racehorses and 'riders for the races' – the first royal jockeys.

Towards the end of the 17th century racehorses were beginning to appear all over the country, with many breeders introducing Arabian stock. Three of these stallions were the sires from which all our thoroughbreds are descended. As the sport began to draw spectator interest, it split into two different categories – flat racing and racing over jumps.

Ideal Downs

Training stables were soon a permanent feature of life in the countryside, but they had to have easy access to large tracts of open downland and grassland over which gallops could be laid for racing practice. As the flinty, chalk soil made this landscape unsuitable for ploughing, the Lambourn Downs were considered ideal terrain for horses to compete with one another and jockeys to sharpen and hone their skills.

Prior to the 1840s horses were treated with little care or compassion. They were taken on long gallops and wrapped in thick rugs to make them sweat. More suitable methods of training were introduced, which enabled trainers to look at each horse individually and assess its potential, fitness level and merit as a future winner.

CHADDLEWORTH

Take a walk on the Lambourn Downs and you'll find it's not just horses and their jockeys who frequent this breezy corner of Berkshire – walkers love it, too. But often you can go there and be completely alone. Other than occasional birdsong and the sound of trees sighing gently in the breeze, there is not a sound to be heard. There are no obvious indications of modern day life – few dwellings, roads or cars. It is difficult to imagine being more remote or cut off from civilisation than here in the quiet rural backwater of the Lambourn Downs – Berkshire's glorious racing country.

WALK 47 DIRECTIONS

❶ From The Ibex take the path opposite the pub, emerging at the next road by Box Hedge Cottage. Keep right and follow the lane between cottages to some steps and a footpath on the right. The grassy path cuts between fields, towards houses. Keep to the right of the village hall and cross the next road to a kissing gate.

❷ Skirt the field, avoid a footpath on the left and continue walking straight ahead beside oak trees. On reaching a gate, go through it and keep a horse paddock on the left. Turn left at the next path junction and keep along the field-edge. Eventually the path broadens out to a track. Over a stile, go straight on at the road and just before it bends right, look for a waymarked track on the left, descending to the extensive buildings of Manor Farm.

③ Cross the road and follow the path up the slope to a stile. Continue ahead, keeping the fence on your left, and make for the brow of the hill. Descend the field slope and make for some bushes in the field corner, concealing two stiles. Head straight down the next field, cross a stile and continue ahead in line with a row of telegraph poles towards the road. Cross a stile and head towards Whatcombe and South Fawley. Turn left at the entrance to Whatcombe, go through the gate and, on reaching the stud, keep left and take the waymarked bridleway.

> ### WHILE YOU'RE THERE
> Extend the walk around the village of Chaddleworth, with its charming cottages and period houses. The church has a memorial to the Nelson family, a member of whom 'fought two dragoons in the Civil War and was never well afterwards', according to the church register.

mobile phone masts and then farm outbuildings. Pass to the right of Henley Farm and follow the byway down to some cottages by the road. Cross to a single track lane and bear left at the next junction.

⑤ Take the first lane on the right and climb steeply to a left-hand bend. Walk along to the next junction, turn right and pass the village sign for Chaddleworth. The church is on the left. Turn right towards Shefford and take the first left path. Look for an electricity transformer, enter a field via a squeeze stile and cross the field, keeping to the right of a large house and alongside a line of trees.

> ### WHERE TO EAT AND DRINK
> The Ibex at Chaddleworth, a Grade II listed building, was originally two cottages. Low ceilings and a cosy log fire add to the charm of the place. Expect a good selection of bar meals and a varied restaurant menu.

④ Climb gradually, keeping to the right of some trees ahead. Where the cinder track bears left, continue ahead on a grassy path to a gate into a wood. Soon through the wood, the path continues along its edge. Descend the bank to a path and turn left. On reaching a track, continue ahead, keeping to the left of

⑥ Cross a stile in the corner and turn left after a few paces at the public footpath sign. Follow the field boundary to the next waymark and drop down to a modern housing development. Turn right at the road and retrace your steps, back to the Ibex.

> ### WHAT TO LOOK OUT FOR
> As you approach the buildings of Whatcombe, look for the striking bronze statue of Snurge who won the St Ledger in 1990. Whatcombe, one of the largest and most successful studs in the area, has produced several winners over the years. The farm stands on the site of a medieval village and there was once a 12th-century church here. When the church was demolished in the 16th century some of the carved stones were incorporated into the farm walls. Little remains of old Whatcombe, but a glance at the map reveals Nun's Walk, which was part of the road system when the village existed.

Combe Gibbet's Grisly Tale

Climb to Berkshire's windswept high ground,
the scene of a 17th-century double murder.

DISTANCE 7 miles (11.3km)	**MINIMUM TIME** 3hrs
ASCENT/GRADIENT 560ft (171m) ▲▲▲	**LEVEL OF DIFFICULTY** +++

PATHS Woodland paths, field and downland tracks, some road and a stretch of Wayfarer's Walk, 6 stiles

LANDSCAPE Gentle farmland, steep scarp of Inkpen Hill and lofty heights of Wessex downs

SUGGESTED MAP OS Explorer 158 Newbury & Hungerford

START/FINISH Grid reference: SU 379616

DOG FRIENDLINESS Signs at intervals request dogs on leads

PARKING Small car park to east of Walbury Hill

PUBLIC TOILETS None en route

Stand at the foot of Inkpen Hill on a bleak winter's afternoon and look for the outline of Combe Gibbet, just visible against the darkening sky. This has to be one of the wildest, most dramatic scenes in southern England. These lonely Wessex downs have a timeless quality to them and nowhere is this more apparent than here at Inkpen Hill.

Crime Scene

The gibbet doesn't look much close up – but one has stood here for more than 325 years. The original gibbet was erected in 1676 following the conviction of a local labourer George Broomham and his mistress Dorothy Newman. The pair fell in love but their plans to be together were complicated by Broomham's wife Martha and his young son Robert.

The couple resorted to drastic measures to get rid of the boy and his mother – lying in wait for them on the crest of the hill. Eventually, Martha and Robert appeared on the scene, out for a walk on the downs. Broomham and Newman sprang an ambush, clubbing them to death with cudgels. It was a most vicious double murder – savage and utterly pointless.

Justice on a Gibbet

Thankfully, the pair were caught and appeared at Winchester Assizes in February 1676. Found guilty, it was decreed that they should be 'hanged in chaynes near the place of the murder'. The execution took place in March that year and it is said that the bodies could be seen hanging from several counties. Vandalism and the elements call for a new gibbet every so often, but successive structures over the years have ensured that the memory of that dreadful, needless incident is kept alive.

Not surprisingly, the events of that winter so long ago became the subject of a film, made in the late 1940s. Written and directed by

COMBE GIBBET

Alan Cooke and John Schlesinger, who was then making his debut as a film director, *The Black Legend* captures the sense of isolation conveyed by this part of Berkshire. Local people were cast in the film which portrayed very effectively the horror of murder and violence in the English countryside.

WALK 48 DIRECTIONS

❶ Cross the road to a gate and go down the field towards the corner of a wood on the right. Edge round it and head for a curtain of trees ahead. Follow the path as it veers to the left of the woodland, making for a gate in the fence. Through a gate walk down the lane to turn left at the bridleway sign. Follow it between fields, sweeping right to Highwood Farm.

❷ Join a concrete track and follow it to the road. Turn left, keep left at the next junction and pass St Laurence's Church. Pass West Woodhay House and a turning for Kintbury and follow the road round a left bend. Turn right 80yds (73m) beyond it at restricted byway sign and continue to Prosser's Farm. Keep ahead at the road, cross over and follow the track to a thatched cottage. Keep right at the first fork and then turn left when you get to the second.

❸ Follow the woodland trail to a junction of paths by a stone and swing left. Keep to the path, skirting the woodland. Emerge from the trees, pass a thatched cottage and turn right at the first kissing gate. Follow the winding path across the field to a kissing gate. Cross the road to a lane and follow it, becoming a stony track, and heading round to the right. Through a gate on the left descend between wire fences to two kissing gates. Cross the field towards Manor Farm and, through a kissing gate, cross the lane.

❹ Follow a path between fences to the right of Manor Farm, then bear right between a hedge and fence, go through two kissing gates and follow sections of boardwalk. Across a footbridge look for a tree house on the right, pass alongside a beech hedge to the road. Bear left signed 'Ham and Shalbourne', and after a cottage to a gate, then a stile, and follow the fence. Cross into the next field via a stile, towards Inkpen church and a stile. Over

the stile, turn right, down to the junction, bear left, pass the Inkpen village sign and swing left to follow a waymarked track. Crossing a step through a stile, continue to the next waymark and then keep a line of trees and bushes on the right before heading out across open fields. Make for the next waymark and keep ahead between the trees.

❺ The path climbs gradually to reach a gate. Through this turn right to a waymark, then go diagonally left, ascending steeply now towards a cleft in the ridge of Inkpen Hill. At the summit, look for a gate in the field boundary and to the right of a pit. Make for another gate ahead and turn left to join a byway. Follow the track to Combe Gibbet and cross two stiles at either end of it. Continue down the track to the road, cross over and follow the Wayfarer's Walk. Keep on the main track, back to the car park.

Combe – Berkshire's Secret Village

Head south from the ridge of Inkpen Hill, making for a tiny settlement hidden below the downs.

See map and information panel for Walk 48

DISTANCE *8.5 miles (13.7km)* MINIMUM TIME *4hrs*
ASCENT/GRADIENT *725ft (221m)* ▲▲▲ LEVEL OF DIFFICULTY +++

WALK 49 DIRECTIONS (Walk 48 option)

At Point **A**, from the car park at the start of the Wayfarer's Walk, follow the lane as it twists and turns down the hill towards Combe. Turn right at the entrance to Wright's Farm and walk along to the farmhouse and outbuildings. Bear left at the waymark and follow the track as it curves back to the road. Turn right to the village of Combe, follow the road round to the right and walk along Church Lane to reach St Swithin's Church, its entrance hidden from view to the left of Manor Farm.

To the right of the entrance to the house is a field with a fine view of the gibbet seen against the skyline. Walbury Hill (974ft/297m), the highest chalk summit in Britain, can be seen from here, blending with the ridge of the downs.

There is no quick or easy way of reaching Berkshire's loneliest village, but that's how it residents like it. St Swithin's Church, in a charming, tree-shaded setting, is one of the county's hidden delights – miles from busy roads and thankfully removed from the hurly burly of the modern world. Work on the church here first began in 1160. The little building has flint walls, a timber tower and a porch dating back to 1652. St Swithin's was restored in 1934, largely through the efforts of a former rector here, the Revd William Hibwood Mowat.

Return to the centre of the village, Point **B**, and turn right for Lower Farm. Pass a postbox and a footpath on the right and keep ahead on the track. Follow the waymarked byway on reaching the buildings of Lower Farm, the track climbing steadily between trees now. Continue ahead at the right-hand bend, passing through a galvanised gate. Follow the bridleway to a fork and veer left to join a sunken path. Over to your left the buildings of Combe can be seen nestling snugly below. Continue to the next fork and keep right. Climb up above clumps of gorse bushes and look for a gate and waymark in the fence corner. Beyond is the car park where both Walks 48 and 49 finish.

Enborne and Britain's Second Line of Defence

Follow the pretty Kennet and Avon Canal to Hamstead Park.

DISTANCE	4 miles (6.4km)
MINIMUM TIME	1hr 30min
ASCENT/GRADIENT	90ft (27m) ▲▲▲
LEVEL OF DIFFICULTY	+++
PATHS	Tracks, roads, estate drives and canal tow path, 1 stile
LANDSCAPE	Lowland country bisected by Kennet and Avon Canal, elegant parkland on south side of Kennet Valley
SUGGESTED MAP	OS Explorer 158 Newbury & Hungerford
START / FINISH	Grid reference: SU 435657
DOG FRIENDLINESS	Under control on canal tow path, on lead in Hamstead Park
PARKING	Car park by Enborne church
PUBLIC TOILETS	None en route

WALK 50 DIRECTIONS

From the car park by the church, turn right and follow the road towards Newbury. Pass Church Lane and, as the road descends a gentle slope, the buildings of Newbury edge into view in the distance. Take the next signposted footpath on the left, at the entrance to Step Up Cottage, and as the drive sweeps left, continue straight on along the track beside Enborne Copse. Follow it across open fields and a stile and soon the Kennet and Avon Canal comes into view ahead. Once over the

bridge, turn left by a pill box and go down to the tow path.

Completed in 1810, the 87-mile (140km) long Kennet and Avon Canal took 16 years to construct. The final bill was in the region of £1 million. With 104 locks and many other impressive features, the canal is regarded as a triumph of engineering.

The Kennet and Avon was built to provide a direct trade link between London and Bristol, thus avoiding the treacherous south coast route which took ships around Land's End. The canal eventually became redundant in the late 1940s but dedicated armies of supporters were determined not to let it die. Restored over many years, the canal was eventually re-opened by the Queen at Devizes in 1990.

Since then it has become one of the south's most colourful and vibrant waterways. But 60 years ago it would have been a very

WHERE TO EAT AND DRINK

A few minutes' walk from the route, towards the A4, lies the Red House at Marsh Benham, offering a quality restaurant and bar menu with such dishes as slow roasted leg of duck, roast fillet of salmon and chargrilled rib-eye steak. The Red House is closed on Sunday evening and all day on Monday.